RAILS THROUGH
BARNSLEY

A PHOTOGRAPHIC JOURNEY

A pair of Class 37 locomotives head a train of empty merry-go-round wagons to Dodworth Colliery in the summer of 1983. The picture was taken from Gawber Road bridge looking back towards Barnsley station and the leafy setting makes it hard to believe that this is just half a mile from the town centre. The train will return loaded with coal for the Aire Valley power stations. The last coal train from Dodworth ran in 1987 and today the line is used only by the Huddersfield-Penistone-Barnsley-Sheffield passenger service.
Alan Whitehouse

RAILS THROUGH BARNSLEY

A PHOTOGRAPHIC JOURNEY

Alan Whitehouse & Peter Rodgers

PEN & SWORD
TRANSPORT

First published in Great Britain in 2016 by
Pen & Sword Transport
An imprint of Pen & Sword Books Ltd
47 Church Street
Barnsley
South Yorkshire
S70 2AS

ISBN 978 1 52670 645 4

Typeset in Palatino by Pen & Sword Books Ltd

Printed and bound by Replika Press Pvt. Ltd

Pen & Sword Books Ltd incorporates the imprints of Pen & Sword Archaeology, Atlas, Aviation, Battleground, Discovery, Family History, History, Maritime, Military, Naval, Politics, Railways, Select, Social History, Transport, True Crime, and Claymore Press, Frontline Books, Leo Cooper, Praetorian Press, Remember When, Seaforth Publishing and Wharncliffe.

For a complete list of Pen and Sword titles please contact
Pen and Sword Books Limited
47 Church Street, Barnsley, South Yorkshire, S70 2AS, England
E-mail: enquiries@pen-and-sword.co.uk
Website: www.pen-and-sword.co.uk

Cover photograph: It is not known whether this was a special occasion, or simply a chance for the local children to have their photograph taken – a rare opportunity in those days. Bob Green

Title page photograph: Wharncliffe Woodmoor 25 July 1960. RCTS Archive

CONTENTS

Staincross Station, looking towards Wakefield Road. Heyday Publishing

INTRODUCTION

BEGINNINGS

An early drawing of Edmunds Main Colliery in Worsborough Dale. A short wagonway took coal to the Worsborough Branch of the Dearne and Dove Canal.

Most people today never handle coal at all. Those who do probably see, or touch it, only occasionally. From being an everyday commodity only a couple of generations ago, coal is now a rarity in most people's lives. But anyone who has ever lifted a sack of the stuff knows what a heavy and awkward product it is. A significant coal industry could never develop unless a cheap and efficient way could be found of transporting it, in bulk, from the pit to the customer. This simple fact is the key to the rise – and fall – of Barnsley's railway network.

The first way of moving bulk coal was by water. In the late eighteenth and early nineteenth centuries, three canals penetrated the Barnsley area, running to basins at Cawthorne, Elsecar and Worsborough, as well as Barnsley itself. But they were only a partial answer to the problem of getting coal to where it was needed: the developing mills, factories and

The statue of Joseph Locke, railway engineer and one of Barnsley's most famous sons. The statue is in Locke Park, Barnsley.

furnaces. The hilly countryside around Barnsley made it hard to plot the course of a waterway.

The answer was to cross the land itself, but on rails rather than the rutted, waterlogged and inadequate roads that existed at the time. The idea of putting things on rails was not a new one even then. It is impossible to say what the first railway was or precisely when it was built, because early tramways developed out of very primitive beginnings, using crude wooden rails and wheels, sometime just to cross a few yards of difficult ground. Initially, tramways were used to link collieries with nearby canals. The well-known illustration of Edmunds Main Colliery at Worsborough is a good example.

But gradually, tramways took on a new identity as small transport systems in their own right, and no fewer than three horse-drawn tramways emerged around Barnsley. The Silkstone Tramway, perhaps the best known, ran on 4-foot gauge tracks from Silkstone

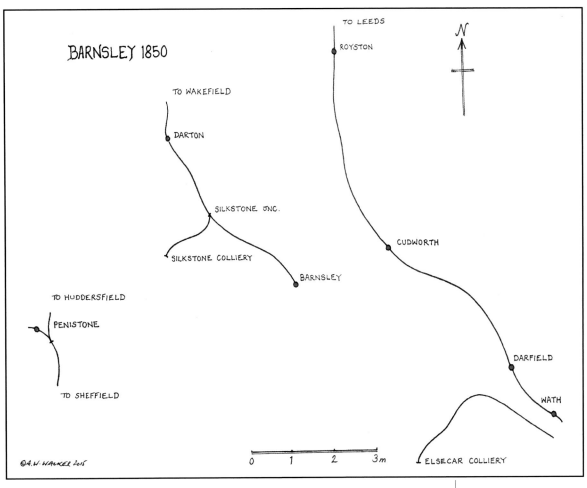

Stone block sleepers on the route of the Silkstone Tramway. These early railways used short lengths of cast iron rail supported on the stone blocks. Wooden sleepers and steel rails – which could be made in much longer lengths – came later.

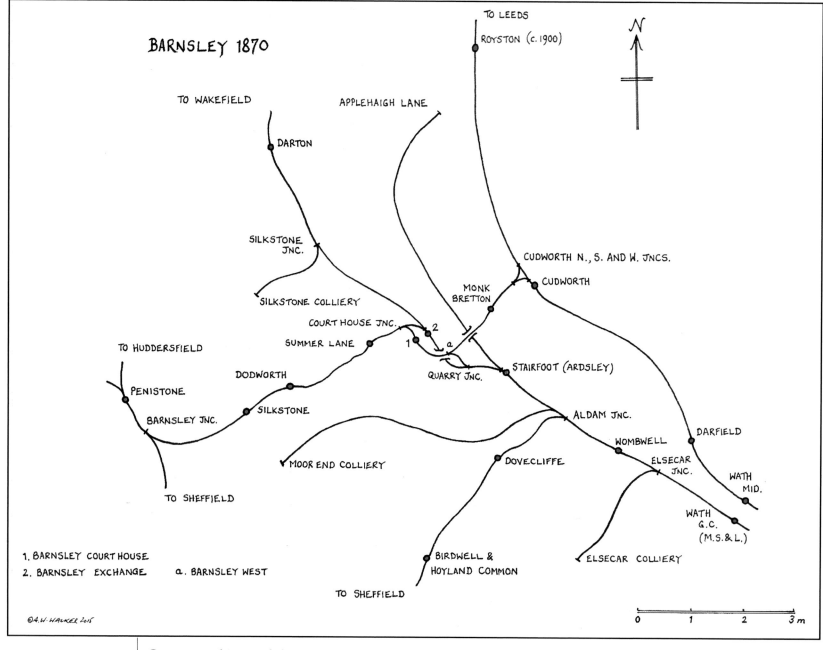

BARNSLEY 1870

TO LEEDS
ROYSTON (c.1900)

N

TO WAKEFIELD
APPLEHAIGH LANE

DARTON

CUDWORTH N., S. AND W. JNCS.

SILKSTONE JNC.

CUDWORTH

MONK BRETTON

SILKSTONE COLLIERY

COURT HOUSE JNC.

SUMMER LANE

2

1

a

TO HUDDERSFIELD

DODWORTH

STAIRFOOT (ARDSLEY)

QUARRY JNC.

PENISTONE

BARNSLEY JNC.

SILKSTONE

ALDAM JNC.

DARFIELD

WOMBWELL

DOVECLIFFE

ELSECAR JNC.

WATH MID.

MOOR END COLLIERY

TO SHEFFIELD

WATH G.C. (M.S.&L.)

ELSECAR COLLIERY

BIRDWELL & HOYLAND COMMON

1. BARNSLEY COURT HOUSE
2. BARNSLEY EXCHANGE   a. BARNSLEY WEST

TO SHEFFIELD

©A.W. WALKER 2015

0   1   2   3 m

Common, taking coal down to Cawthorne Basin where it was loaded onto canal barges. The first section opened in 1810 and lasted fifty years before being abandoned as the mines it served were worked out.

Just over ten years later, the Worsborough Tramway opened, again linking coal and ironstone mines around Rockley and Pilley with the Dearne and Dove Canal basin at Worsborough Bridge. This was a more ambitious

system, several miles in length, which divided at Rockley into two main routes, using a 4' 3" gauge. Another 'first' was a short tunnel at Rockley, which can still be seen today. This system had a surprisingly long life, finally

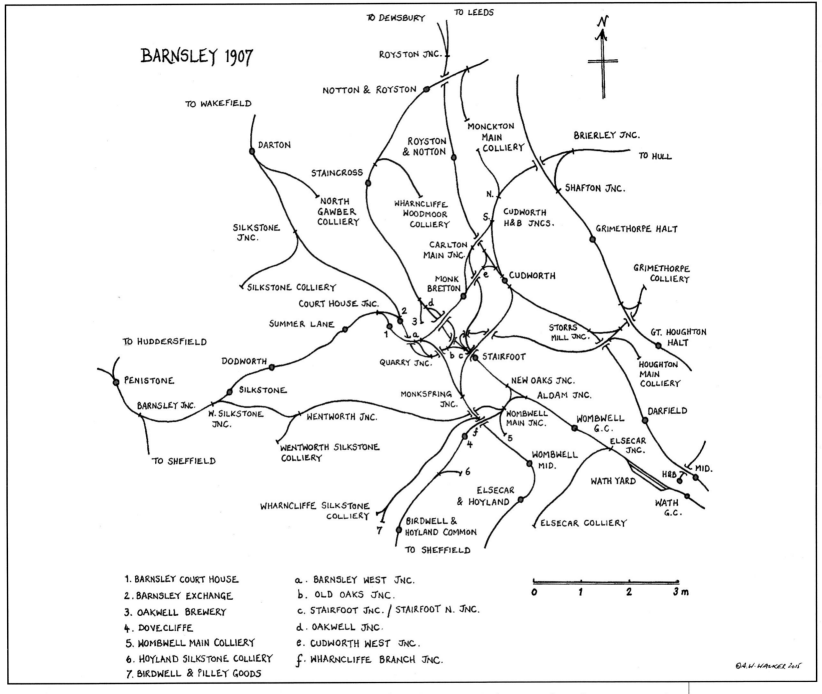

BARNSLEY 1907

TO DEWSBURY
TO LEEDS
ROYSTON JNC.
NOTTON & ROYSTON
TO WAKEFIELD
DARTON
MONCKTON MAIN COLLIERY
ROYSTON & NOTTON
BRIERLEY JNC.
TO HULL
STAINCROSS
SHAFTON JNC.
NORTH GAWBER COLLIERY
WHARNCLIFFE WOODMOOR COLLIERY
N.
CUDWORTH H&B JNCS.
GRIMETHORPE HALT
SILKSTONE JNC.
S.
CARLTON MAIN JNC.
GRIMETHORPE COLLIERY
SILKSTONE COLLIERY
MONK BRETTON
e
CUDWORTH
COURT HOUSE JNC.
2
d
SUMMER LANE
3
STORRS MILL JNC.
GT. HOUGHTON HALT
TO HUDDERSFIELD
1
a
QUARRY JNC.
b c
STAIRFOOT
HOUGHTON MAIN COLLIERY
DODWORTH
NEW OAKS JNC.
PENISTONE
SILKSTONE
MONKSPRING JNC.
ALDAM JNC.
BARNSLEY JNC.
W. SILKSTONE JNC.
WENTWORTH JNC.
WOMBWELL MAIN JNC.
WOMBWELL G.C.
DARFIELD
TO SHEFFIELD
WENTWORTH SILKSTONE COLLIERY
f
ELSECAR JNC.
5
WOMBWELL MID.
MID.
H&B
WATH YARD
4
6
WATH G.C.
WHARNCLIFFE SILKSTONE COLLIERY
ELSECAR & HOYLAND
7
BIRDWELL & HOYLAND COMMON
ELSECAR COLLIERY
TO SHEFFIELD

1. BARNSLEY COURT HOUSE
2. BARNSLEY EXCHANGE
3. OAKWELL BREWERY
4. DOVECLIFFE
5. WOMBWELL MAIN COLLIERY
6. HOYLAND SILKSTONE COLLIERY
7. BIRDWELL & PILLEY GOODS

a. BARNSLEY WEST JNC.
b. OLD OAKS JNC.
c. STAIRFOOT JNC. / STAIRFOOT N. JNC.
d. OAKWELL JNC.
e. CUDWORTH WEST JNC.
f. WHARNCLIFFE BRANCH JNC.

0   1   2   3 m

©A.W. WALKER 2015

being abandoned in about 1920. Over forty years later, when the M1 motorway was driven across the former line of route, a store of wooden wagon wheels and other artefacts were uncovered.

The third route, the Elsecar and Thorncliffe Tramway, left another branch of the Dearne and Dove Canal at Elsecar and ran to Milton, serving an ironworks, at Hoyland and on to Thorncliffe,

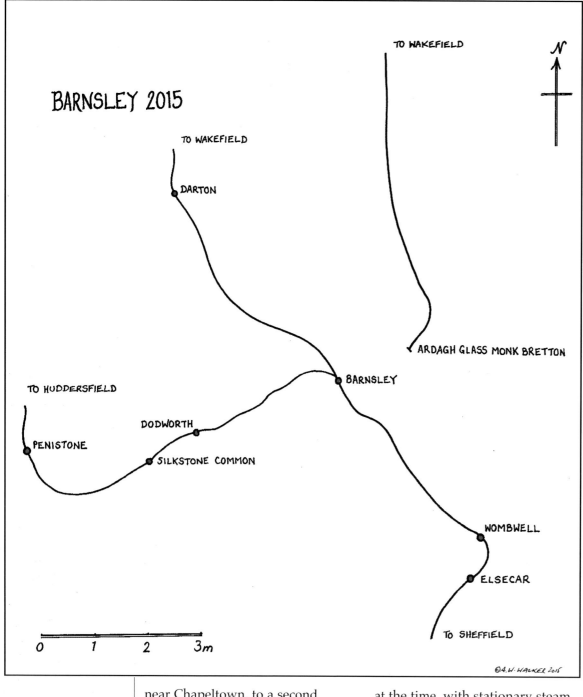

BARNSLEY 2015

TO WAKEFIELD

TO WAKEFIELD

DARTON

TO HUDDERSFIELD

PENISTONE

DODWORTH

SILKSTONE COMMON

BARNSLEY

ARDAGH GLASS MONK BRETTON

WOMBWELL

ELSECAR

TO SHEFFIELD

0   1   2   3m

©A.W.WALKER 2015

fifty years later in 1880. However, another section survived and was rebuilt as a standard gauge railway, which was used as a colliery branch line until just before the First World War.

These developments combined to make this area of South Yorkshire one of the most industrially advanced in the country and, compared with roads and canals, it allowed the rapid transport of coal in significant quantities. But, impressive as they were, these tramways did no more than set the stage for the next phase: the development of one of the most dense railway networks in Great Britain. A system that had Barnsley at its heart and which was driven almost entirely by King Coal.

near Chapeltown, to a second ironworks. A number of coal mines were included in the scheme. This used what was high technology at the time, with stationary steam engines hauling sets of wagons up one of the gradients. It opened in 1830 and part of it was closed

CHAPTER ONE

BARNSLEY... OR NOT?

I f you were the adventurous sort and decided that this new-fangled rail travel was for you, then back in those early days, your rail journey from Barnsley began not with a steam locomotive, but with a horse bus. Any luckless travellers who came to the town only found out when they stepped onto the platform, that the station marked 'Barnsley' on their map was in fact at Cudworth: three miles from the town itself. The horse bus provided that vital link.

This was far from unusual in the early days of railways. Locomotives were primitive and, relatively speaking, underpowered. The most famous of all railway builders, George Stephenson, insisted that his lines should have no gradient steeper than 1 in 100. The North Midland Railway, which laid those first tracks through Cudworth, was started in 1836 with the aim of linking Derby and Leeds. It gives an idea of how inflexible Stephenson was that he not only refused to build his railway through Barnsley, but even bypassed Sheffield as well, because of the engineering work that would have been needed to keep the route relatively flat.

Cudworth station on a September day in 1966. The locomotive is an 8F Class, 48641, and it comes with an interesting history. Although designed by William Stanier for the London Midland and Scottish Railway, it was actually built at the Southern Railway workshops in Brighton in 1943 as part of the war effort. It was withdrawn from service three months later. The station itself is deserted because by this time local passenger services had been axed. Steve Armitage Collection

But fourteen years earlier Cudworth was a hive of activity as enthusiasts turned out in their scores to see a railtour hauled by two veterans: on the left a Class D20 locomotive, 62360, built by the North Eastern Railway, and on the right 40726, another 4-4-0 passenger engine, but this time built by the Midland Railway.
J W Armstrong/ ARPT Collection

The railway opened for business in 1840 and within three years, Cudworth was the scene of an accident when a train running several hours late smashed into the rear of another passenger train standing in the station. One passenger was killed and many more were injured. An inquiry found the driver to be inexperienced. He was an employee of George Hudson, the so-called 'railway king', who had bought out the North Midland Railway and then sacked the regular drivers who had objected to him cutting their wages.

The station was renamed Cudworth in 1854 after two other companies had built lines into Barnsley itself. The Leeds and Manchester Railway opened a route from Wakefield through Haigh and Darton, which ran to Exchange Station making an end-on junction with the South Yorkshire Railway's new line from Doncaster and Mexborough.

Cudworth then became just another station along what had become the Midland Railway's main route from London to Derby, Sheffield, Leeds and Carlisle. And, although a diversion route was built into Sheffield, Barnsley never quite made it onto the main line, having to be content instead with a link line between the town centre and Cudworth, over which a two-coach shuttle service ran until the 1950s. This service was affectionately known as either the 'Cudworth Flyer' or more simply, the 'Pusha' (it was usually a push-pull train in which the locomotive stayed at one end, either pushing or pulling the train).

The route through Cudworth grew in importance. The tracks were quadrupled and Cudworth Station became an imposing place, with four platforms and a large range of buildings. Traffic was heavy and Cudworth gradually became the focus of a complex system of main lines and colliery branches. A second railway, the Hull and Barnsley, also ran passenger and goods trains, while a little way north at Royston, a locomotive shed was established to

Two more views of 62360 at Cudworth. The railtour ran in August 1952 and the crowded platforms are an indication of how significant a pastime railway enthusiasm was. Almost every schoolboy collected engine numbers and special trains, and tours hauled by unusual or historic locomotives would quickly sell out. *J W Armstrong/ ARPT Collection*

A very wet June day in 1957 and Class C14 locomotive 67448 arrives at Cudworth with the famous 'Cudworth Flyer', the shuttle service that linked the main line with Court House station in Barnsley town centre. By this time the Flyer was into its final few years. When local passenger services through Darfield, Cudworth and Royston were ended, there was no point in running the Flyer any longer.
J F Sedgwick/ARPT Collection

provide engines to move increasing tonnages of coal. At its height, the shed had a substantial allocation of locomotives, almost all of them dedicated to coal traffic.

Royston was also intended to become a major junction on the Midland Railway system. A short way to the north of the town itself, the route split. One arm ran towards Leeds, while the other was the start of what was intended as a new line to Bradford and then on to the existing line to Carlisle. The intention here was to cut a few miles off the London-Carlisle journey time, thus speeding up services in what was a very competitive market.

Alas, this new line reached Dewsbury and then stalled for lack of money and traffic. In some cases work began and was then stopped as it became clear that the line did not have the future originally hoped for it. The village of Crigglestone, near Wakefield, would have had

Fast forward to 1984 and it is obvious that the railway is becoming rundown. This view of Cudworth North shows diesel locomotive 45 017 passing redundant sidings with what appears to be a train of coke – it is piled high on the hopper wagons because it is less dense that coal and could be heaped up without exceeding the 21-ton loading limit of the wagons. Vaughan Hellam

its own station: the platforms were excavated but never built. The line went into steady decline from the 1950s and closed completely in 1968.

The main line to Leeds prospered, carrying Anglo-Scottish express trains, sleeper services, mail and express freight along with Leeds-Sheffield local trains and, of course, coal. However colliery closures during the 1960s, the rundown and closure of the Hull and Barnsley line, which fed traffic onto the main line, and the loss of goods traffic to road lorries, all

combined to reduce the importance of the line north of Sheffield. The Cudworth Flyer struggled on until 1958 when it finally lost the battle with the bus, which was almost as quick and more convenient for most people.

In 1968, Royston, Cudworth and Wath North stations all closed their doors for the last time, as all passenger trains over the route were axed. The station at Darfield had closed five years earlier. The express trains were diverted away because of the speed restrictions enforced as a result of mining

subsidence, which had slowed the trains down to an unacceptable degree. Just three years later, Royston's locomotive shed closed along with Carlton North Sidings and the Hull and Barnsley Railway's yard at Cudworth. What was left was a freight-only route, which saw nothing more than a handful of Summer Saturday holiday trains and occasional diversions.

Two years later saw the start of a saga which would see Barnsley's first railway reduced to little more than a long siding serving a couple

Long after passenger trains disappeared, coal traffic kept the railway through Cudworth open and here we see a pair of Class 20 locomotives, 20 112 and 20 210, on a typical train in 1981. Vaughan Hellam

of local industries. Initially, all looked promising: the 1968 decision to divert all passenger trains over an alternative route was reversed, and some regular passenger services began using it again. Expresses running from the North-East to the South-West provided the main traffic, and British Rail began spending heavily on the line to raise speeds and accelerate the trains: there was talk of trains running at 115 mph between Scotland, Newcastle, Sheffield, Birmingham and Bristol.

There were even suggestions of a new 'Cudworth Parkway' station, an idea being trialled by BR at the time, in which a basic station was surrounded by extensive car parks, thus allowing a quick and easy interchange between car and train. But it all came to nothing. By the early 1980s, BR was in a round of spending cuts as its Inter-City business was told by the government at the time to cut costs and pay its

A rare colour picture of steam at Royston shed. This view was taken in December 1966, just a few months before the last steam locomotives at Royston disappeared. The engine in the foreground is an 8F, 48553.
G Turner/ARPT collection

When they reached the end of their working lives some locomotives were used as stationary boilers, producing steam for heating or cleaning purposes. That is what has happened to this B1 Class locomotive. The running number has been removed and a 'departmental number' – 32 – has been crudely applied. G Turner

own way instead of relying on a subsidy. In 1982, all passenger trains were re-routed again.

Soon after, the line was severed at Wath Road Junction, leaving, in effect, a long branch line from the north to serve coal loading plants at Royston Drift, Grimethorpe and Houghton Main collieries, along with sand trains to the Redfearn National Glass works at Monk Bretton and the Monckton Coking Company's works at Royston. The national miners' strike of 1984/5 marked the end of another era, with a never-ending round of pit closures. By the early 1990s all three coal loading plants had closed as coal production was wound down.

This left the line dependent on two flows of traffic: to the coke works and to the glass factory. By now it was no more than a single track, which saw only two trains per day. The coke works closed in 2015, ending yet another traffic flow and leaving the line's future dependant on the trains carrying sand to the glassworks.

Much of the original line of the route has now disappeared and it is uncertain how much longer even the remaining fragment of Barnsley's first railway will remain

8F locomotive 48707 standing on the shed. These engines were the mainstay at Royston for years and were among the last steam engines to be based there.
G Turner/ARPT collection

A landscape that has changed out of all recognition: a freight train approaching Royston station in June 1967. RCTS Archive

Another all-purpose locomotive seen around Royston and Cudworth was the ex-LMS 2-6-0 'Crab'. They got their unusual nickname because of the ungainly appearance of the valve gear. RCTS Archive

Anyone trainspotting around Barnsley in the 1950s and '60s would be certain to come across an ex-Midland Railway 4F like 43983. They could be found doing almost any job though, in this area, hauling coal was the usual day's work. RCTS Archive

A little north of Royston itself was Royston Junction where lines to Leeds and Dewsbury diverged. A Wartime built Austerity or WD locomotive, 90351, is caught on camera with the inevitable coal train. The date is July 1966 and the engine would be scrapped a little over a year later. Steve Armitage Collection

Steam locomotives consumed huge amounts of coal – and this had to be loaded onto tenders and bunkers. The huge piece of equipment seen on the left in this view of Royston shed is designed to lift a complete wagon and tip the contents into a coal hopper from where it was loaded onto locomotives. B1 61131, 6 September 1966. Steve Armitage collection

Locomotive 43076 makes light work of a short coke train at Royston. The picture dates from September 1966 and steam was almost finished. The dirty, unkempt condition of the locomotive says it all. Steve Armitage collection

A trio of pictures of the railway at work at Royston. An Austerity 2-8-0 locomotive with its inevitable coal train is in the top view, middle is an ex-LMS 'Black Five' mixed traffic locomotive 45080 with an express freight and, bottom, a newly-built diesel locomotive, D7582 (later known as Class 25) meets an Ivatt Class 4MT steam locomotive. Steve Armitage Collection

A BR Standard Class 9F stands amid the clutter of Royston shed. Steve Armitage Collection

Whilst just outside the shed building itself, a trio of ex-LMS 8F engines are ready and waiting for their next job. Steve Armitage Collection

Detail of the complex system of rods and cranks that both couple the driving wheels, transmit power from the cylinders to the wheels and operate the valve gear which admits steam into the cylinders and then lets it out as exhaust. Steve Armitage Collection

An ex-Midland Railway 2P locomotive, 48501. These engines were often used on the local service between Sheffield, Darfield, Cudworth, Royston and Leeds, and that would explain its presence at Royston. The piece of tarpaulin tied over the chimney indicates that it is out of use and in store. Bob Green

A 9F gets its train on the move at Royston in July 1967. By this time steam power was on its last legs. Steve Armitage

Although local passenger trains were an early victim of nationalisation, long-distance express services continued to use the route until the 1980s and this view of Royston Junction shows an Inter-city 125 High Speed Train crossing onto the Leeds route in 1982. Andrew Walker

Royston Junction, looking south with 'Black Five' 45208 on a train of coal empties. Train spotting provided a good day out for many people in those days! The piers of the former Barnsley Coal Railway can be seen in the background, and, further away still, Monckton Colliery and the coke works. B A Jordan

CHAPTER TWO

COAL IS THE KEY

Few things in life were simple when 'Railway Mania' took hold in Victorian times. There were in fact two separate booms in railway building, and at almost any location that looked remotely interesting to the railway promoters, it could be guaranteed that a raft of competing schemes would appear, all jostling for the Parliamentary approval needed before building work could begin.

Barnsley was no exception to this and the 1840's railway boom saw so many competing ideas put forward that it took the best part of a decade to sort the wheat from the chaff. The first to come to fruition, the Barnsley-Wakefield line, had its origins in a scheme to link the North Midland Railway – whose route as we have seen ran through Cudworth and Royston – with the Leeds and Manchester Railway.

The route would leave the North Midland line at Wincobank, just north of Sheffield, and run through the town and on to Horbury, near Wakefield, before linking into the Leeds and Manchester line. In the end, the project was split into two halves and the northern half, linking Barnsley with Wakefield,

Coal was the key, but it also brought with it many other associated industries that generated traffic and rapidly expanded Barnsley's railway system. Coke was one, and this picture shows Barugh Coke Works, one of many small coking plants built across the town.
Old Barnsley

was the one which was pushed ahead first. The builders faced a significant obstacle between Haigh and Crigglestone, where a 1,745 yard tunnel was needed to pierce the ridge of land separating the Dearne and Calder valleys. But construction work went well and the whole line from Horbury Junction to Barnsley opened for business in 1850.

Coal, as ever, was the key to the new line's success and traffic grew so rapidly that the original single track had to be doubled; a job that was completed by 1855. However, there was no money to add a second track at the single bore Crigglestone Tunnel, and it

remained a bottleneck until 1902 when the Lancashire and Yorkshire Railway – as the Leeds and Manchester had by now become – opened a second tunnel alongside the first. The route quickly settled down to an existence that changed little for decades, with local trains running from what became known as Barnsley Exchange station – on the same site as today's station – and serving three village stations at Darton, Haigh and Crigglestone. At Horbury, the trains took the Lancashire and Yorkshire main line to Wakefield's Kirkgate station.

The southern half of the original scheme, to Sheffield, was also completed and will be described in

a later chapter. Until 1960 the two halves were operated as completely separate services, and anyone wanting to travel from the south of Barnsley to Wakefield needed to change not only trains, but stations, arriving at Court House but departing for Wakefield from Exchange. An announcement by British Railways in 1959 paved the way for major changes, when a major remodelling scheme at Quarry Junction would create a direct Sheffield-Barnsley-Wakefield link using Exchange station, which itself would be rebuilt.

A new train service was launched in 1960, using new diesel trains and running from Sheffield to

A 1950's view of Barnsley's engine shed. Under the British Railways coding system, it was known as 36D – 36 was the district number, in this case Doncaster, and the letter indicated the shed's place in the local hierarchy. Exchange station is on the left. It had only platform until the shed was closed and demolished in 1959.
FW Hampson/ARPT Collection

Gordon Turner/ARPT Collection

There was a healthy traffic in holiday excursion and special trains right into the 1980s. In this August 1962 view we see a special departing in the Sheffield direction. What is slightly unusual is that the locomotive, 48709, is a Class 8F freight loco, not normally used on passenger trains. Perhaps there was a shortage of engines that day!

Barnsley, Wakefield and Leeds. At the same time, the village stations of Haigh and Crigglestone were closed, which helped to speed the service up. In essence the same service operates today, but with the addition of a long-distance Leeds-Nottingham service, calling only at Wakefield, Barnsley and Sheffield. In some ways the town is better connected than it ever has been as a result of the changes.

Goods traffic over the line was always predominantly coal. It served a string of collieries and threw off a branch to Silkstone which passed under the Barnsley-Huddersfield road at Barugh Green, traces of which can still be found today. A second scheme, which came to nothing, would have linked the line at Darton with the branch line to Clayton West. This would have created a route from Huddersfield to Barnsley, although admittedly a long way round. However like many other railway schemes, it sank without trace and

only the first few hundred yards were built to serve a coal mine. Some of the mine buildings are still intact today close to the centre of Darton.

The line also served Woolley Colliery and in the late 1970s, this was chosen as the site for a high capacity loading plant. Here, coal would be wound to the surface from across a large part of the Barnsley Coalfield and loaded into what BR called 'merry-go-round' trains. These used new hopper

wagons that could be loaded and unloaded with the train still on the move and were used to transport coal to power stations. The National Coal Board claimed the project would transform the economics of the coalfield and turn a lossmaker

into a profitable operation.

The scheme envisaged a 34-wagon train carrying around 1,300 tonnes, which would leave Woolley every half hour. Two huge concrete loading bunkers were built along with new sidings, but it was

A picture that is not all it seems. The B1 locomotive is carrying headlamps for a train of empty carriages, so this may have been a holiday train terminating at Barnsley with the empty stock being taken on to Sheffield for cleaning. The date is August 1962. The tracks into the loco shed, closed three years previously, can be seen.
Gordon Turner/ARPT Collection

Another holiday train, this time powered by a Black Five mixed traffic engine, 45589, again in August 1962. When Exchange station was rebuilt, the second platform was long enough only for the new local diesel trains – which can be seen on the right. Longer trains heading towards Sheffield had to cross over to the opposite track to use the long platform and then cross back.
G Turner/ ARPT Collection

barely completed when the mining strike changed things forever. In the wake of the strike, Woolley Colliery itself closed, leaving only the coal preparation and loading plant in use, meaning that far fewer trains used it than had originally been planned. The second wave of pit closures in the early 1990s saw the loading plant made redundant and the bunkers were subsequently demolished in a series of controlled explosions. This was not quite the end, because as the whole Woolley site was redeveloped, the waste heap was excavated and useful amounts of coal were taken away

by train. The site is now occupied by houses with coal mining and the rail connection just a memory.

The frenzy of 'Railway Mania' meant that it was almost inevitable that there would be more than one route between towns the size of Barnsley and Wakefield. Barnsley was now a boom town, with new coal mines being sunk and a sizeable support industry – making mining machinery and other equipment – growing on the back of it. So, hard on the heels of the first route, plans were laid for a second railway to Wakefield. But it became bogged down by legal wrangling

over buying the land needed to lay the tracks through Staincross, Notton and Ryhill.

It was eventually built stage by stage, with the initial aim of tapping coal traffic from pits at Wharncliffe Woodmoor and Monckton. It began life as the Barnsley Coal Railway, which had an alliance with the South Yorkshire Railway, which itself was building yet another line into Barnsley, but this time from the south. The Coal Railway ran to a junction with the SYR's main line at Stairfoot, allowing the coal trains to bypass the town centre and take the SYR route towards either Doncaster or Sheffield.

Two shots of locomotives at Barnsley shed. Both still carry their pre-nationalisation numbers, 9325 and 9303, even though the pictures were taken in 1949 – well over a year after British Railways was formed. Both are Class N5 0-6-2 tank engines, built for hauling coal traffic short distances from coal mines to sorting sidings. Barnsley shed always had a dozen or so to hand.
K H Cockerill/ARPT Collection

Two more shed views which must have been taken one Sunday in 1957, because this was the only day of the week when they were all gathered together. Barnsley had so many allocated locos that, when the shed yard was full, they were stored in a siding next to the CEAG building. The upper view shows a row of J11 0-6-0 locos and the lower a pair of rebuilt Class 04 2-8-0 types.
F W Hampson/ARPT Collection and A R Thompson ARPT Collection

As Barnsley shed was run down before being closed completely, lines of redundant steam engines were stored, waiting to be taken for scrapping. With the CEAG building in the background we can see a Class C13 tank engine, 67445. Someone has chalked GCR (Great Central Railway) on the side of the tank along with its former GCR number. Behind it is a Class 04. The bent running plate suggests a heavy shunt and that might be why this engine has been condemned.
A R Thompson/ARPT Collection

This first section opened in 1863 and ended in the middle of nowhere, near Notton. Several attempts to finance an extension to Wakefield failed and it became known as the 'Barnsley stump'. It was not until 1882 that the Manchester, Sheffield and Lincolnshire Railway – which by this time had taken over the SYR – managed to obtain both the land and the Parliamentary powers needed to extend further north. In addition, a new tightly curved and severely graded line was laid in near Barnsley Main Colliery to give passenger trains direct access to Court House Station. In September of that year a new passenger service was launched between Barnsley, Wakefield and – for a time – Leeds.

But passenger trains were never the reason that this line was built and it saw only a modest

Two more pictures of Barnsley shed stalwarts, an N5 tank engine and a J11 tender engine. Both were intended for shifting coal and general purpose work. Down the years, Barnsley was home to dozens of them.
A R Thompson/ARPT Collection

C J B Sanderson/ARPT Collection

service before becoming an early casualty of road competition, with the Yorkshire Traction Company's buses finally seeing off the trains in September 1930. However, the stations survived longer and were used occasionally by excursion trains for another twenty years or so. Every year, the combined Royston working men's clubs would charter several trains for their annual trip to the seaside, which would leave from Notton and Royston station on the Coal Railway, so as to avoid congesting the main line through Royston itself. The line was also used in the summer months to transfer empty coaches between Leeds and Sheffield for the summer Saturday holiday trains.

By the 1960s, the end was in sight for the Coal Railway. Some of the collieries it had served were closed and others could be served

No. 67434 was something of a celebrity locomotive at Barnsley. The C13 tank spent most of the 1950s based here, operating passenger trains to Penistone, Doncaster and Sheffield. D Fairley/ARPT Collection

by alternative train services. Just as it was built, it was closed stage by stage. In 1965 it was severed and cut back, with the two ends being operated as separate branch lines.

Cutback followed cutback until, by the mid-1970s, the last few hundred yards from the junction at Stairfoot were being used for storing surplus coal wagons. There was an attempt to

stir up interest in relaying the tracks as a tourist steam railway, but this was unsuccessful, and today the old trackbed is used as a footpath along the Dearne Valley Country Park.

Most locomotives at Barnsley spent their lives wearing an overcoat of soot, oil and general dirt. J11/3 64442 looks as though it is just back from overhaul and a repaint, looking splendid in shiny black paint. It was selected for rebuilding with a superheated boiler and piston valves, which can be seen poking out beneath the smokebox. It is also fitted with steam heating gear for working passenger trains. The picture dates from 1957. Steve Armitage Collection

The well-known level crossing gates at Jumble Lane have been replaced by barriers in this 1970's view of a special leaving the station headed by a Class 47 locomotive. Bob Green

In 1960 British Railways completely reworked the passenger service through Barnsley, creating a new Sheffield-Barnsley-Wakefield-Leeds route. It was operated from the start with brand new diesel units. A train of two three-coach units is seen at Barnsley Exchange Junction as it approaches from Wakefield. L A Nixon

The trees are in full leaf, so this must be a summer holiday excursion train at Willow Bank, approaching Barnsley Exchange station. The locomotive is an ex-LMS 2-6-0 'Crab', a versatile engine, which gained its nickname because of the ungainly looking operation of the valve gear and coupling rods. B A Jordan

The cameraman has turned and is looking the other way, towards Barnsley town centre, in this shot of a coal train, doubtless from either Woolley or North Gawber collieries and equally doubtlessly heading for Wath Yard where the wagons will be sorted for their individual destinations. The locomotive is an ex-Great Central Class 04 2-8-0.
B A Jordan

A trio of pictures showing industrial tank engines at work at North Gawber Colliery. The NCB was a major user of steam power and the final NCB locomotives were still running at mines around Barnsley until the 1970s. Tom Heavyside/Bob Green (bottom right)

North Gawber Colliery yard was just yards from the village and the grimy tank engine – a wartime austerity design bought by the NCB – and ramshackle wagons contrast with the bungalows just over the boundary fence. This scene changed completely with the closure of the colliery. Tom Heavyside

It is 1955 and this 0-4-0 saddle tank engine, named *Woolley,* is still going strong at Woolley Colliery after fifty-three years of service. RCTS Archive

Another austerity tank engine, this time at the colliery screens at Woolley. The locomotive was built by the Hunslet Engine Company for war service and scores were bought for industrial use afterwards. RCTS Archive

Almost every colliery
had at least one
locomotive of its own
and usually a small fleet.
This one, another 0-4-0
saddle tank, is pictured at
Darton colliery screens in
August 1959. RCTS Archive

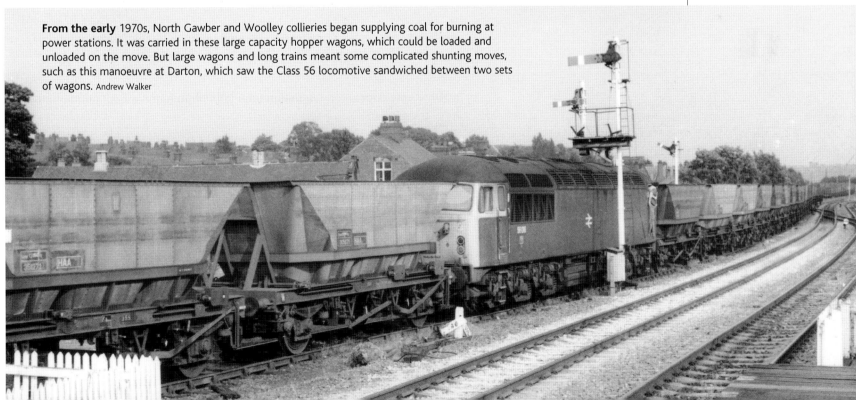

From the early 1970s, North Gawber and Woolley collieries began supplying coal for burning at
power stations. It was carried in these large capacity hopper wagons, which could be loaded and
unloaded on the move. But large wagons and long trains meant some complicated shunting moves,
such as this manoeuvre at Darton, which saw the Class 56 locomotive sandwiched between two sets
of wagons. Andrew Walker

Darton station, with a Sheffield to Llandudno train being hauled by a Class 31 locomotive, 31 102. Andrew Walker

Two more views of Darton station. On the left, a Class 56 shunts merry-go-round wagons bound for North Gawber Colliery. On the right a Class 108 diesel unit runs into the platform, bound for Sheffield.
Andrew Walker

This veteran locomotive was built by the Lancashire and Yorkshire Railway around the turn of the century and is seen here in 1955 still doing the job it was built for at Crigglestone Colliery, which was served by the Barnsley-Wakefield line. RCTS Archive

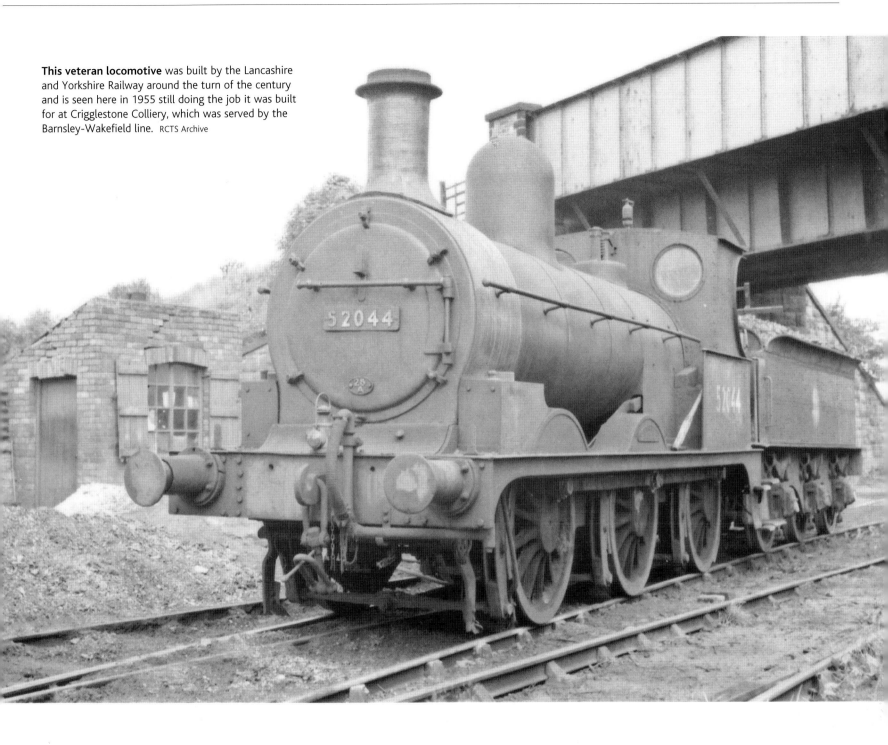

Woolley Colliery was chosen as a concentration point for loading 'merry-go-round' hopper trains under a new system of loading and unloading trains on the move, taking bulk coal from pits to power stations. Heading towards Woolley Colliery with a train of empty mgr hoppers is a Class 56 locomotive. The train is passing through Crigglestone Junction where the line to Huddersfield once turned off the Barnsley-Wakefield route. Junction, signalbox and hopper wagons are all now railway history but some Class 56 locos soldier on.
Alan Whitehouse

The other route to Wakefield, the Barnsley Coal Railway, really was about coal rather than passengers. The stations were modest wooden-built affairs and the passenger service gave in to bus competition in the 1930s. But coal traffic surivived into the 1960s. These pictures show Staincross and Notton and Royston stations.
Heyday Publishing

CHAPTER THREE

A RAILWAY FOR SOUTH YORKSHIRE

Even as the first railway promoters were building southward from Wakefield, a second company was already hard at work on its own route into Barnsley. Coal was once again the key, and this time the South Yorkshire Railway was hoping to tap coal traffic from collieries along the Dearne Valley, with a line running into Doncaster and the Great Northern Railway's main line to London.

The South Yorkshire Railway would grow to become one of the main players in creating the railway network around Barnsley, building two key routes and throwing off branches in all directions to link itself into every new coal mine that it possibly could.

The SYR main line was built stage by stage, with access to collieries driving the decisions

The South Yorkshire Railway line ended at Barnsley's Exchange Station, which it shared with the Lancashire and Yorkshire Railway's line from Wakefield. Moving slowly across Jumble Lane Crossing, just a few yards from the end of the SYR, is Class B1 locomotive 61165, which at the time was allocated to Mexborough shed and would have often been seen around Barnsley.
H K Boulter/Author's Collection

A little further away from the town centre, Class 04 locomotive 63883 hauls a heavy freight train past Freeman's Coal Yard, just off Pontefract Road. The engine was allocated to Barnsley shed at the time.
Steve Armitage Collection

An impressive picture of a Class 8F locomotive 48113 standing at Stairfoot No. 2 signalbox. The signaller appears to have been having a conversation with the driver – and is definitely not in BR uniform! The picture dates from 1962 and shows a scene that has changed utterly. B A Jordan

about what to build next. As the line gradually crept northwards through Mexborough to Wath, instead of heading straight for Barnsley, a branch was built to Elsecar in order to serve new collieries. The line then went to Wombwell, where a second branch went off to Worsborough Dale (again to exploit coal traffic), and finally Stairfoot. It reached Barnsley Exchange station in 1851, which it shared with the Lancashire and Yorkshire service to and from Wakefield. This was an interesting arrangement: the two companies formed what is known as an end-on junction, where the tracks simply meet each other in a seamless junction. In this case it was half-way along the platform at Exchange. Trains could have run direct from Wakefield to Doncaster via Barnsley, but this never happened.

Passengers were very much a side issue for the SYR. It ran straight through the eastern side of the coalfield, where new reserves were being discovered almost daily, and by the time it was taken over by the Manchester, Sheffield and Lincolnshire Railway, the SYR served over seventy collieries. This is why the line had no trouble securing the finance needed to build it: local landowners, the newly-emerging industrialists and local dignitaries, led by Earl Fitzwilliam, were almost queuing up to put up their cash. One of the company's early locomotives was named after the earl and he had his own private station at Elsecar, which today forms part of Elsecar Heritage Centre.

A short time after the line was complete, the Great Northern Railway began running a Barnsley

One traffic that has lasted longer than coal on Barnsley's network is sand for the glassworks that used to be dotted around the town. This 1983 picture shows a Class 31 diesel locomotive shunting hopper wagons into Beatson Clark's works near Stairfoot. Vaughan Hellam

The complex junction at Stairfoot. Railways went off in all directions from this point – it was also as close as the Hull and Barnsley Railway ever got to the town itself. The Midland Railway's line to Cudworth is carried overhead on the girder bridge. J H Meredith

The most famous locomotive in the world, *Flying Scotsman*, storming through Stairfoot with an enthusiasts' special train in 1969. It was the first and only time the locomotive passed through Barnsley.
L A Nixon

to Doncaster passenger service. It was an erratic affair (the first timetable does not actually give any train times), and it took almost ten years for any coherent timetable to emerge. Even that amounted to just four trains each way per day. Trains called at a string of village stations including Stairfoot, which was emerging

as a major railway junction, and Wombwell.

By all accounts the SYR was a happy-go-lucky affair, where neither safety nor scruples were worried about too much. Within a short time, a train had smashed through the level-crossing gates at Jumble Lane, right next to Exchange station, because the driver was new and did

not know it existed and the crossing keeper had failed to open the gates because the engine did not sound the usual warning whistle. Driver training and proper signals to warn of hazards ahead appear to have been luxuries that the SYR's directors thought they could manage without.

In another affair that ended up in the town's courtroom, a passenger

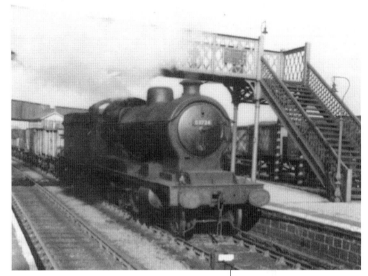

Class N4 and N5 tank engines were a mainstay of Barnsley's railway system for fifty years or more, working coal wagons to and from pits and shunting almost anything from one siding to another. This one was caught on camera at Stairfoot. Bob Green Collection

named Walker was travelling to the town in 1851 when his carriage broke away from the train at Stairfoot and began running back towards Wombwell. Walker jumped for his life and was badly hurt. He sued for damages and the SYR's astonishing defence was that passengers were warned not to leave carriages whilst they were in motion! The judge was having none of it and the SYR paid out £30 compensation.

A class 04 locomotive, No 63714, running through Stairfoot station in 1958. By this time, the station was only a year away from total closure, having already lost its service between Barnsley and Sheffield. David Green

Stairfoot sat in a valley bottom, so when runaways occurred, the resulting smash usually happened somewhere in this area. There were a string of accidents down the years, often caused because most freight trains had no continuous brakes on the wagons, just a handbrake, which could not be applied when the train was moving. It was only the efforts of the locomotive brakes and the guard in his van at the rear of the train that kept things under control. This picture shows the results when that system went wrong. But the practice of unbraked freight trains – particularly coal – was not abandoned until well into the 1980s. John Goodchild Collection

The same steep gradients meant that passenger trains often needed a helping hand. Barnsley shed's 64404 – a Class J11 locomotive – is at the head of this passenger train assisting Class B1 61175 at Pindar Oaks. Bob Green Collection

But in other ways the company was on a roll. The coal industry was now expanding rapidly

and the SYR promoted a line to link Barnsley with Sheffield, leaving the Doncaster route at Wombwell and climbing up the Dove Valley through Dovecliffe and Birdwell to a summit near Pilley, where it crossed into the

Blackburn Valley for the run down to Sheffield through Westwood and Chapeltown. This line was characterised by its sharp gradients of around 1-in-60 and was difficult to build. The SYR took on the project in 1846, but it was 1854 before the first trains covered the complete route.

Part of the delay was caused by a last-minute change of plan. The original idea had been for a lengthy tunnel running northwards from just before the summit at Pilley. Trains would have left Westwood station and plunged underground, taking a straight line to emerge close to the Cock Inn at Birdwell. Some earthworks can still be seen today, showing how the line would have emerged from the tunnel and run straight onto an embankment to cross Birdwell Dike and the carriage drive to Stainborough Castle.

The tunnel had been largely dug,

Another Class 04 locomotive at the head of a coal train at Quarry Junction. Bob Green

The South Yorkshire Railway ran on to Doncaster via Wombwell and Mexborough. It was taken over by the Manchester, Sheffield and Lincolnshire Railway, which in turn became the Great Central Railway. The architecture in this view of Wombwell Central station is unmistakeably MS&LR/Great Central. Heyday Publishing

with teams working outwards from ventilation shafts along the line of route, with only the entrances to be dug out and completed. But the SYR was persuaded to change its plans and divert the line down the Dove Valley instead, so as to serve new collieries at Pilley, Birdwell, Hoyland and Barrow Main, between Worsborough and Dovecliffe. The tunnel was abandoned and the luckless contractor refused payment. He sued and won £55,000 – a colossal sum in those days.

Diverting the line allowed two stations – at Birdwell and Dovecliffe

While at Mexborough, the loco shed dominated the railway scene. This picture gives some idea of the scale of operations there with scores of locomotives all needing coal, water, maintenance and repair. K H Cockerill ARPT

The South Yorkshire Railway also threw off a second line at Aldam Junction, Wombwell, which ran to Sheffield via Birdwell and Chapeltown. Although it originally formed an important link in the emerging railway system, it became something of a backwater, taking a long and meandering route to Sheffield to avoid tunnelling. The passenger service ended in December 1953, and here, Barnsley Shed's C13 Class 4-4-2T locomotive 67409 is seen pausing at Dovecliffe in the summer of that year with a Barnsley-Sheffield train.
W A Camwell/Stephenson Locomotive Society

– to be included, though neither of them was conveniently sited. Dovecliffe was a good half-mile walk from Worsborough Dale and Birdwell was built half a mile from the village at the insistence of the Earl of Wharncliffe. This was one of the larger stations along the line and included a glass portico to allow the earl to leave his carriage and board a train without getting wet. Inconvenient stations were a feature of this railway: Westwood, next along the line after Birdwell, was in the middle of nowhere, and Chapeltown was right on the edge of the village. This goes some way to explaining the sparse passenger service, which did not begin until

1855. This was several months after the line had opened to coal trains, and the passenger trains that did run can never have been used by any great numbers. From a timetable of seven or eight trains a day in the 1930s, the service had shrunk to just two per day when it was finally axed in December 1953.

But this did not matter at the time. The SYR was about coal traffic and the new route was so busy that it quickly became clear that the original single track would need doubling. The only place where trains could pass each other was at Westwood, where two 'travelling porters' were based. One of them had to accompany every train between

Westwood and either Sheffield or Barnsley to ensure that two trains never got onto the same stretch of track. It was a clumsy and inefficient way of running a railway, but it was 1876 before the second track was laid and better signalling installed.

The line originally ran to a junction at Aldam, which faced away from Barnsley and towards Doncaster, meaning that all passenger trains had to stop and reverse at Wombwell. A new chord line to complete the triangle was opened in 1879, allowing passenger trains to swing to the left at Wombwell Main to a junction at New Oaks and thus on to Stairfoot and Barnsley.

Twenty years later, and looking in the opposite direction, there is little left of Dovecliffe station apart from the signalbox – which will itself soon be replaced by the new building behind it. From here the track has been singled for the 2 miles or so to Rockingham Colliery, Birdwell, where the line was severed in 1966 when the M1 motorway was built. An English Electric Type 3 (later Class 37) locomotive makes its way towards Wath Yard with a train of loaded coal hoppers. The signalman is waiting to collect the single-line train staff – used to make sure that only one train at any time was allowed onto the single track to Rockingham. Alan Whitehouse

Dovecliffe station and signalbox were something of an oddity. The signalbox was built as a three-story extension tacked onto the end of the stationmaster's house. By the early 1970s the rest of the station had been demolished. The box itself was in a poor state but was needed not only to signal trains, but to control the level crossing. BR built a brand new box to replace it – but then found there was no equipment available to control the crossing gates! It stood empty for around seven years until the gear could be found. Alan Whitehouse

With these improvements in place, the line settled down to an unspectacular existence. As already discussed, passenger services were never important and the line

was never a direct route between Barnsley and Sheffield, as it took 20 miles to cover the journey as opposed to the 14 miles it took by road. Almost all the freight carried was coal, lifted from the string of collieries that ran almost the length of the line. After 1907, much of this was worked to the large Concentration Yard at Wath, where coal trains were marshalled either to go to Immingham Docks for export, or across the Pennines to the

industrial areas of Lancashire.

Yet taken together, these two arms of the South Yorkshire Railway were an attractive – and lucrative – piece of railway, and it was not long before larger companies began taking an interest. The Manchester, Sheffield and Lincolnshire Railway eventually struck a deal to take a 999-year lease on the SYR, including its interest in the Barnsley Coal Railway, which, as we have seen,

The most important station along the route was Birdwell. Larger than the others it also had a large glass canopy at its entrance, built so the Earl of Wharncliffe did not get wet when changing from his carriage to the train. Birdwell and Hoyland Common, as it was known, was also built at Tankersley, again for the Earl's convenience. Here is a classic Edwardian view with the many station staff on display.

Looking towards Barnsley at around the time the line lost its passenger trains. W A Brown/Author's Collection

After the regular passenger service ended, the line was still used for excursions and diversions. This enthusiasts' special ran in the late 1950s, headed by Mexborough Shed's Class B1 61165. It passes through a different Birdwell station: the footbridge, platform awnings and lamps have gone and tufts of grass are colonising the platform. The final excursion train passed through here in 1959. H K Boulter/Author's Collection

had a direct link into the SYR system at Stairfoot. The core stretch from Aldam Junction to the yard at Wath became so busy that the twin tracks were doubled again to four, and the MS&L Railway built a small locomotive shed at Barnsley, opposite the single platform Exchange station.

The MS&L Railway changed its name in 1898, becoming the Great Central Railway. The name may have changed, but the pace of change did not. The Great Central was a progressive, forward-thinking company and continued making improvements to the way the coal traffic – still growing every year – was handled.

The culmination came in 1907 when a new marshalling yard,

known as Wath Concentration Yard, was built at Wath-upon-Dearne. The site was chosen because the land there was relatively flat and there was space available to lay out a grid of sorting sidings in both directions. It was also a central point in the South Yorkshire coalfield: it is said that at its height, Wath yard was handling coal from 107 collieries.

Two huge sets of sidings were provided, each with a shunting hump to allow rapid sorting and remarshalling. The wagons within each train would almost certainly be heading for different destinations, and the main job at the yard was to sort them into trains all heading for the same place. So, a loaded coal train straight from one of the

collieries would arrive, and the final destination of its wagons noted before the wagons for each destination were uncoupled from their neighbours. The train was then pushed over the shunting hump by a specially-designed heavy tank engine that had been built for the job. As each set or 'cut' of wagons rolled down the other side, they freewheeled and were directed into a siding allocated for their destination. When a complete train for a given destination had been created, it was taken off, freeing up the siding for the creation of the next train.

The sidings were controlled by power-operated points, allowing sidings to be switched very rapidly, speeding up the rate at which wagons could be handled.

No 67409 again, this time at Birdwell with its Barnsley-Sheffield train in the summer of 1953. The elderly carriages are interesting, one from the Great Northern Railway, one from the Great Eastern, complete with clerestory roof – used for gas or oil lamps in the days before coaches were lit by electricity. In the background is the volcano-like spoil heap of Rockingham Colliery. W A Camwell/Stephenson Locomotive Society

It amounted to a revolution in coal handling and for a few years Wath was the only example of its kind on any British railway. The trick needed to be repeated with empty wagons, because at the time most coal wagons were owned by the coal companies and needed to be returned to their 'home' colliery. The railway companies merely acted as hauliers. It was a complicated and time-wasting business, but the GCR had made the best of a bad job.

This was almost a high water mark for the South Yorkshire Railway's creation: coal trains were always the most important traffic by a wide margin. Barnsley's locomotive shed housed perhaps three dozen locomotives. All but three or four at any given moment were there to work the coal traffic. There was little doubt about the pecking order: coal trains might be unglamorous, but they paid the bills. Also, there were usually three tank engines at the shed, which were used to work passenger trains over the Penistone-Barnsley-Doncaster and the Barnsley-Sheffield lines. Whilst passenger trains to Sheffield were a very local affair with just a couple of elderly carriages, that first Barnsley-Doncaster service was incorporated into a new Penistone-Doncaster timetable and became altogether more prestigious. Some trains ran all the way to and from Cleethorpes and, as the number of trains grew, the MS&L struck an agreement with the Midland Railway to build a new station, Court House, which will be described later. One overnight

The South Yorkshire Railway also threw off another, shorter, branch line to Elsecar to tap the lucrative coal traffic. This line ended at what is now the Elsecar Heritage Centre. It never carried regular passenger trains, but at the heritage centre visitors can still see Earl Fitzwilliam's private station, used to carry him and his guests to Doncaster Races. These two views show an enthusiasts' special arriving at Elsecar in 1953. The locomotive is an ex-Great Central Railway 'Director' D11 Class, No 62667, named *Somme* in commemoration of the First World War battle. K H Cockerill/ARPT Collection

service, principally for carrying newspapers, ran from Manchester to Cleethorpes.

This comfortable existence began unravelling with the closure of the Sheffield passenger service in 1953. The route it took was indirect and slow and, as noted above, the stations were almost without exception, inconvenient for the places that they were meant to serve. Within six years the Penistone-Doncaster service had also been chopped and Court House station closed, although both routes remained busy with the coal trains they had been built to carry, for a few more years at least. In 1966 Wharncliffe Silkstone Colliery

at Pilley was closed at short notice and, instead of building a bridge to carry the new M1 motorway beneath the line at Birdwell as originally planned, the decision was taken to close it completely between Rockingham Colliery and Smithywood Colliery at Chapeltown.

The remaining 'stump' from the Barnsley end of the line still served two collieries: Rockingham and Barrow Main, as well as a coke works, also at Barrow. But Rockingham closed in 1974 and the line was cut back, again, to Dovecliffe. Barrow itself closed in 1986 and, thanks to the general run down of the coal industry, this was

the final source of traffic over the remaining line back to Wath Yard and it was all closed. In the same year, Cortonwood Colliery, just a short distance from the yard, also closed and the branch line serving it dismantled. This, in turn, paved the way for the closure of Wath Yard.

The first SYR line from Barnsley to Doncaster fared little better. Coal traffic slowly dwindled and the section from Stairfoot through Aldam to Wath became less and less important. The quadruple tracks were cut back to two in 1974 and this was followed in 1981 by closure of the route from Wath to Penistone and Manchester. At a

Along the way the Elsecar Branch served Cortonwood Colliery, famous as the mine which sparked the 1984/85 miners' strike. Getting empty wagons in and loaded ones out of Cortonwood involved some complicated shunting and the crew of this Wath-based Class 37 take a long and careful look to make sure their route is clear. The date is January 1982.
Alan Whitehouse

The South Yorkshire Railway built its way into the Barnsley coalfield from Doncaster, passing through Mexborough and Wath. By the early 1970s steam had ended and the Class 37 diesel locomotive had become the mainstay for working coal trains. This one is seen at Wath with a classic haul of coal.
Tom Heavyside

stroke, this removed much of the remaining traffic and the line was cut back again to a single track that divided at Aldam, with a branch to Dovecliffe and another to Barnsley. However, this was little used and

taken out of service leaving, as described above, only the line to Dovecliffe generating any traffic.

There have since been several proposals to re-instate a Barnsley-Doncaster train service, using the old line of route. But all have come to nothing; the expert view being that too few people would be likely to use the trains. Much of the route has since been built over and Wath

Yard is now a combination of nature reserve, housing and light industry, with call centres being a major employer.

The SYR was built to carry coal: all else was something of a sideshow, so when the coal industry declined and eventually died, it was almost inevitable that the railway built to exploit it would die with it.

The SYR branch to Sheffield was, as already described, cut in two in 1966. One arm ended at Rockingham Colliery, while at the Sheffield end, the line ran to Smithywood, where a coke works kept the railway to Meadowhall and Tinsley open for another twenty years. Steam also reigned here in the shape of industrial tank engines used to marshall the train before they were taken away by BR locomotives. The whole scene is a wonderful evocation of a heavy industrial past that has now all but disappeared.
Tom Heavyside.

CHAPTER FOUR

THE MIDLAND RAILWAY STEPS IN

With competition so intense, it seems odd that a second railway link to Sheffield should have taken so long to appear. But it was not until 1897 that Barnsley's second link with the city was finally complete and carrying passengers. The mighty Midland Railway had been eyeing up a more direct Barnsley-Sheffield route for some time and so created the line that is still in use today.

It had already been possible to travel by railway between the two places ever since the Barnsley to Cudworth link had been established. However, this was a roundabout route and involved changing trains from the main line onto the 'Cudworth Flyer' and the Midland Railway wanted something better. Not to mention the fact that the company had its eye on the coal and other freight traffic that might be on offer.

It began by extending what had previously been a primitive tramway to the Thorncliffe Ironworks at Chapeltown.

EX-London Midland and Scottish Railway 2-6-2 tank engine No 41274 is departing from Court House station with the 'Cudworth Flyer' push-pull service. This was one of the two services the Midland Railway (which became part of the LMSR) launched as part of its expansion into Barnsley. B A Jordan

The other was the second line to Sheffield. The Midland route was much more direct than the South Yorkshire Railway, partly because the decision was taken to drive a tunnel between Wentworth and Hoyland Common station and Chapeltown station. In 1988 a Barnsley-Sheffield diesel unit is running towards Wombwell. The pronounced dip in the route at this point was needed to allow the line to dive under the South Yorkshire route. The bridge abutments which once carried it over the Midland line can be seen.
Alan Whitehouse

Immediately to the north, Tankersley Tunnel was driven, emerging near the village of Harley, where a station known as Wentworth and Hoyland Common was provided. From here the route reached Elsecar and then Wombwell, before leaping across the Dove Valley by means of the Swaithe Viaduct and on into Barnsley via Kendray. It gave the Midland Railway a 16-mile route, as opposed to the South Yorkshire Railway's 20 miles, and easier gradients into the bargain.

It was so well-built that part of it became a relief line for the Midland's main line from Sheffield to Leeds, through Cudworth. A link opened in 1899 and ran from Monk Spring Junction, between Swaithe and Kendray, before cutting across country and swinging over the junctions of Stairfoot on a lengthy

A rare view of shunting taking place at Monk Bretton. The locomotive is an ex-Midland Railway 2F, 43250. J Sedgwick/ARPT Collection

bridge to Cudworth Station South Junction, where trains then regained the main line to the north. Its purpose was to allow express passenger and fast freight trains to bypass bottlenecks at Swinton and Rotherham. Known as the Chapeltown Loop, it carried some of the Midland's most important services, including the London to Glasgow 'Thames-Clyde Express'.

Lower down the scale of

In addition to driving the line into Barnsley, the Midland Railway also created a link to the main line at Cudworth, creating a second fast route between Sheffield and Leeds via Chapeltown rather than Wath. Until the late 1950s, express services were timetabled to use this line and here a BR Standard Class 5 locomotive, No 73002, crosses the substantial girder bridge at Stairfoot. Bob Green

priorities, local trains ran between twelve and fifteen times per day, the timetable changing little down the years. Royston shed supplied tank engines for the job, which was far from demanding, as most trains were just two coaches long and were often worked as push-pull trains, where the locomotive stays at one end of the train, alternately pushing and pulling the carriages. All of these local services ran between Sheffield's Midland Station and Barnsley Court House. Along with the Barnsley-Cudworth service, and the fact that it owned the London-Carlisle line which passed through Cudworth, this gave the Midland Railway a commanding presence in the town and, as we shall see, it was to become the key player in providing a new and better station.

The new line was not short of traffic. At Chapeltown, a spur was driven into the Thorncliffe Ironworks, which down the years had developed into a range of industries, including production of the famous Izal brands of toilet paper and disinfectant, the latter essentially a by-product of the coke production needed for iron smelting. A new colliery at Skiers Spring, near Hoyland Common, provided more traffic, but the Midland had yet another trick up its sleeve.

Looking enviously at the string of collieries, coke works and other industries along the Dove Valley, the company decided to build its own branch line to rival the South Yorkshire Railway. From a junction between Wombwell Station (it became known as Wombwell West to avoid confusion with Wombwell Central) and Swaithe Viaduct, a single track branch line snaked

Another view of the 'Flyer' with an Ivatt tank locomotive, 41273, at its head. The engine would have been based at Royston shed. The picture dates from 1951.

The most prestigious train to use the Chapeltown loop for several years was the 'Thames-Clyde Express' – the crack London to Glasgow service from St Pancras. It is pictured here racing towards Stairfoot with an unidentified 'Jubilee' Class locomotive in charge. B A Jordan

The new junction allowed trains from both Sheffield and Doncaster to use the original South Yorkshire Railway's line into Exchange station, and here Class 55 'Deltic' locomotive 55 003, named 'Meld' after a famous racehorse, powers past the site of Freeman's coal yard in Pontefract Road with a special in July 1978. This is the only time a Deltic locomotive has visited Barnsley. L A Nixon

up the valley, never more than a few hundred yards away from the original SYR line, and very often running right alongside it, all

In BR days the two lines from Sheffield were rationalised, creating a new junction on the site of the existing Quarry Junction, allowing trains from the Midland route to get into Exchange Station. This paved the way for a new Sheffield-Barnsley-Leeds service and allowed the closure of the lines through Court House station. For such a pivotal piece of railway equipment, Quarry Junction signalbox was a very modest looking place. J H Meredith

the way to Wharncliffe Silkstone Colliery at Pilley.

Connections were laid in to all the same collieries and other industries and the Midland Railway and the Great Central Railway (as the SYR had by this time become) were locked in a battle for the available traffic. It was hugely counter-productive because colliery owners could now play one company off against the other, bargaining for lower and lower rates, which ate into the

Two views of Wombwell station in the 1980s. Originally known as Wombwell West to distinguish it from Wombwell Central on the opposite side of the town, it is by now simply Wombwell and is also unstaffed. Andrew Walker/Alan Whitehouse

railway companies' profit margins. In spite of this, both lines remained open until after nationalisation in 1948, when British Railways quickly closed down the Midland branch. It was a less convenient line to operate: locomotives had to be sent all the way from Royston shed to work the trains and the junction itself faced the Sheffield direction. On the original SYR route, trains ran straight down the valley to the junction at Aldam

and then on through Wombwell to the concentration yard at Wath: an altogether simpler way of getting the coal on its way.

The Midland's Barnsley-Sheffield line saw few changes until the post-nationalisation rationalisation programme. It sat at the heart of the proposed changes to Barnsley's passenger services, with its trains diverted away from Court House station via the remodelled Quarry Junction, events which are described

A vintage view of Elsecar and Hoyland station. Once, both here and Hoyland had goods sidings and a signalbox that between them might have provided a dozen or so local jobs. Today it is unstaffed but busier than it has ever been with commuter traffic to both Sheffield and Barnsley.
Heyday Publishing

in the chapter on Barnsley's stations. New diesel trains took over from steam in 1958 as BR tried to change the image of the railway from being slow, dirty and sooty to something faster and more in tune with the era of 'you've never had it so good'. Wentworth and Hoyland Common station closed in 1959, around the same time that a Leeds-Barnsley diesel service also started. In April 1960, the two ends of the service were joined and a direct Sheffield-Barnsley-Wakefield-Leeds timetable launched.

In 1967 the line lost its main line status with the closure of the Monk Spring-Cudworth link. In 1970, the remaining stations were de-staffed, as British Rail introduced what it called Paytrain, where guards collected fares on the move, like a bus.

The next milestone came in 1983 with the diversion of Huddersfield-Penistone-Sheffield trains via the route. Freight traffic gradually disappeared from the line as collieries closed, while other traffic

was either lost to road haulage or disappeared completely. The Thorncliffe complex, for example, no longer exists. The final regular freight was, aptly enough, coal. When the Woodhead Line was closed in 1981, coal from Dodworth Colliery needed an alternative route. Trains ran several times a day from there down the line to Barnsley and on to Wincobank on the outskirts of Sheffield. From here the train reversed, heading off to the power stations of the Aire Valley. The final train ran in December 1985 and since then, the route has been passenger-only.

However, in one of the many twists and turns of transport history, a new system of funding and managing local rail services meant that South Yorkshire's newly-formed transport authority took over responsibility for funding and running the line. It worked in partnership with British Rail, which acted as a sort of haulage contractor, running trains to a

timetable specified by the transport authority and then issuing it with a bill for the cost of doing so, minus the money collected from fares.

The timetable was gradually improved to the point where a half-hourly service ran virtually all day. The Huddersfield-Sheffield service added a third train per hour and, more recently, a Leeds-Nottingham service has begun using the line, calling at only Wakefield and Barnsley before reaching Sheffield. The line was also re-signalled and is now operated entirely from a control panel at Barnsley. In many ways, all these developments mirror what has happened over the national railway network: freight is now just a memory, and the route simplified with sidings and so on removed. The passenger service that it left behind runs more frequently, reflecting the national trend for people to travel further to find work. The future of the line, in contrast to many others around the town, now seems secure.

Like every other railway in the Barnsley area, the Midland line to Sheffield served a string of collieries and other industries. The last working colliery on the line was at Skiers Spring, near Hoyland Common, and well after steam locomotives had ceased operating on the main line, its small industrial tank engines continued marshalling coal trains and that is what is happening here as a train of merry-go-round hopper wagons is prepared for dispatch to one of the Aire Valley power stations.
Tom Heavyside

Local trains could be a hit-and-miss affair, with none of the regular interval timetables passengers enjoy today. An ex-LMS 2-6-2 tank engine, probably from Royston shed, is ready to re-start with its three-coach load from Chapeltown South station to Barnsley Court House in March 1949.
W A Camwell/Stephenson Locomotive Society

CHAPTER FIVE

ONE TOWN – TWO STATIONS

In a rational world, a town the size of Barnsley would never have had two railway stations. But the Victorian era of 'Railway Mania' was anything but rational: rival companies fought tooth and claw for the best routes, the best station sites and the best sources of potential traffic.

We have already seen how two companies thought it worth building rival routes to both Wakefield and Sheffield. Something similar happened in the town centre itself, with rival railways setting up their own operations in order to better frustrate their competitors, or even to prevent their competitors frustrating them.

Sometimes this duplication could be born out of complaints over a poor or inadequate service. There were certainly many complaints about Barnsley's first railway station, Exchange, which as we have seen, opened its doors in 1850.

It might be thought that the town's residents would be glad of a new station right next to the town centre, instead of having to take a 3-mile journey by horse bus to catch their train. But not a bit of it.

The town council set the tone from the start, complaining about 'that disgraceful and beastly hole called the railway station'. The Sheffield, Rotherham, Barnsley, Wakefield, Huddersfield and Goole Railway, which opened the station, should perhaps have paid more attention to the grumbling, with the state of the station even being debated in Parliament by 1863.

Among many other complaints, the MPs heard that the size of the ladies waiting room was such that 'one lady of modern dimensions would occupy a very considerable portion of it.' The railway company remained deaf however, and little or nothing was done to improve matters. During the Parliamentary debate on the bill authorising construction of Barnsley's second station, Court House, it was said that 'under no combination of circumstances could the accommodation be worse' than at Exchange.

As we have seen, Exchange became a joint station very early in its life, with the South Yorkshire Railway's Doncaster trains sharing the single platform with the trains to Wakefield; a situation that remained for twenty years or so. A second station, across the town at Summer Lane, was the terminus for a line to Penistone and Manchester. The promoters were puzzling on the best way of getting from there into the town itself, and were for a time thwarted by the difficult topographical conditions and how to build a line with the easiest possible gradients.

Exchange station was far from ideal. When the SYR added trains to Sheffield to its timetable in 1855, the solitary platform was handling three separate services: it was clear that something had to be done. However, it was to be another fifteen years before Court House station opened for business in 1870, with every train service into the town, excepting those from Wakefield, switching to it almost overnight.

The Lancashire and Yorkshire Railway, which was by now the owner of Exchange, had made an eleventh hour offer to upgrade and expand it, perhaps with an eye on the income it could make from charging other companies to

use it. The offer fell on deaf ears, though the Manchester, Sheffield and Lincolnshire Railway, which had by now bought the South Yorkshire Railway, did retain the rights to use the station and run trains through it to reach the line to Penistone. However, they were rarely exercised except by freight services.

If all this looks like a failure of common sense, then that is also how it looked to many of the town's dignitaries at the time. There were several attempts to create a central or union station for the town, and

Court House played host to both London Midland and Scottish Railway services to Cudworth and Sheffield, and London and North Eastern Railway trains to Penistone, Doncaster and Sheffield. This immediate post-war picture shows an ex-Midland Railway 0-4-4 tank engine – designed for exactly this sort of work – arriving at the station with either the Cudworth Flyer or a local from Sheffield. The engine would have been based at Royston shed. *Bob Green Collection*

the attempt that made the most progress came with the Hull and Barnsley Railway's plan to run right into the town centre. But both the Hull and Barnsley's ambitions and the hopes for one central railway terminal came to nothing, and Barnsley ended up with two

Court House and Exchange stations were linked by a stretch of steeply graded track at the start of the line to Penistone. In the summer of 1962 a 'Jubilee' class locomotive tackles the climb away from Exchange with the Weymouth-Bradford holiday train. This was the last regular steam-worked service through the town. In the background is the site of Barnsley loco shed, by now demolished. But, oddly, footplate crew were still based here and locomotives parked up between duties. A pair of Brush Type 2 (later Class 31) diesels stand waiting for their next job. L A Nixon

stations sitting side by side.

Today, Court House is the site of one of Barnsley's largest car parks, but when it opened for business in 1870, it was seen as by far the better station. It was well placed: the two rival routes to Sheffield could both use it and the line from Penistone ran straight into its platforms, allowing the start of a Penistone-Barnsley-Doncaster service, as well as providing access to the 'Cudworth Flyer' too. The Midland Railway, which operated one of the routes to Sheffield and the line out to Cudworth, was largely

responsible for the construction, creating a neat and compact station with three platforms. It took its name from the old courthouse building, which had been bought to provide a booking office, waiting rooms and staff accommodation. Always known in the town as 'top station', Court House led a remarkably quiet existence. There was no grumbling about the facilities and no major incidents happened there. Just months after it had opened, however, it was the starting point for one of Barnsley's more spectacular railway accidents.

A different day, but the same train, heading from Weymouth-Bradford running via Penistone, Huddersfield and Halifax. The locomotive is a Black Five, No 45643 and the gradient, as it begins the slog up to Penistone, is obvious. L A Nixon

In addition to the passenger station, both the Midland Railway and the Manchester, Sheffield and Lincolnshire Railway had goods yards on the same site, and it was from the MS&L Railway's yard that ten wagons began running out of control down the gradient towards Stairfoot. Signalmen in boxes along the route could only watch helplessly as the wagons gathered speed with the steepening gradient. With no facing points to divert the runaways, all ten wagons stayed on the track until they ran into a passenger train standing in Stairfoot station. The impact killed fifteen and injured a further fifty people.

Court House quickly settled into a pattern of services that altered little down the decades. This was

Only a comparatively small amount of freight passed through Exchange station. One of the regular workings was the sand train for Beatson Clark's glassworks, already pictured in Chapter 3. This view shows locomotive 37 052 with the train in October 1983. Vaughan Hellam

before the days of regular interval or 'clockface' services, so anyone wanting to travel needed to know the timetable, for trains departed at all kinds of odd moments. Court House also became the main station for special trains and excursions, either to the coast or to Doncaster Races or perhaps Belle Vue pleasure gardens in Manchester.

After 1923, when the railway companies were grouped into the 'Big Four', both Barnsley stations were operated jointly by the London, Midland and Scottish Railway and the London and North Eastern Railway. One result of this was that signalmen at both stations had to satisfy inspectors from each of the two companies before they could be signed off as competent – a bit like having to sit the same exam twice!

Nationalisation of the railways in 1948 meant that changes were inevitable. Duplication was seen as costly and wasteful and one early result was the decision to axe the former LNER's Sheffield via Birdwell service in 1953. But this was just the prelude and British Railways was working on plans for major changes around Barnsley. The full scheme was finally unveiled in 1959, and involved the closure of Court House station, which was by now under-used. In addition to the Sheffield service, the Cudworth 'Flyer' was axed in 1958 and the Penistone-Doncaster service a year later, leaving Barnsley with two stations each handling just one service: to Sheffield via Elsecar and the other to Wakefield. The complex tracks at Quarry Junction were to be remodelled, creating a through route from Sheffield to Barnsley

Exchange and thus on to Wakefield and Leeds, with new diesel trains providing a seamless service straight through the town.

British Railways had also claimed that the Court House viaduct, which carried trains above the bus station and around the edge of the town centre, was in need of urgent repairs costing £200,000 – a large sum at the time. However it was an unpopular decision, with many people echoing the comments of a century earlier and complaining that the facilities at Exchange were far inferior to those at Court House. With the remodelled tracks, and the plan to run a new Sheffield-Barnsley-Leeds service, Court House was simply

in the wrong place. The inevitable happened on 15 April 1960, when the final Court House to Sheffield train departed, before the new service via Exchange took over. Four days later, on 19 April, Court House was officially closed.

This was not quite the end, however. Although the viaduct was closed and the tracks severed at the platform ends, Court House remained open for parcels trains and freight from the goods yards, although this traffic had to be worked via Penistone. The last trains ran at some time in the mid-1960s, and by 1970, all of the tracks had been lifted. Today, little of the old station survives apart from the

former courthouse itself, which is now a bar and restaurant.

Exchange – by now called simply 'Barnsley' after the closure of Court House – quickly settled down to its new existence. Part of the rebuilding work had involved demolishing the engine sheds and making space for a second platform. The new Quarry Junction involved a steep link between the route into Exchange and the Midland line to Sheffield, but this presented no problem to the diesel trains. Quarry Junction also became the point where the routes to Sheffield and Doncaster diverged, simplifying what had been a complex tangle of tracks.

Class 37 No 37019 hauls a train of four Class 76 electric locomotives through Exchange in 1981. This was the year the electrified line from Wath and Wombwell to Penistone and on to Manchester – the Woodhead Line – finally closed. The locomotives were occasionally hauled through Barnsley if an incident on the electrified route prevented them from using it.
Vaughan Hellam

A view which few will now remember: Exchange station and the loco shed when steam power still ruled. The station has just a single platform – the only regular service to use it was the Barnsley-Wakefield shuttle – and the shed occupies the rest of the site. Judging by the number of locomotives stabled in the shed sidings, this may have been a Saturday afternoon or Sunday when the endless coal trains were stopped for a few hours. The year is 1957.

Through the 1960s and into the first half of the 1970s, the daily service was supplemented by Summer holiday trains and excursions with Llandudno, Blackpool, Weymouth and Scarborough being some of the more popular destinations. The 1970s were essentially a decade of decline: the motorway network allowed more aggressive coach competition for daily travellers, while the holiday services suffered as more families bought their own car and an improving road system cut journey times, meaning the trains were less competitive. One by one the holiday services disappeared, the last to go being the Weymouth train in 1986. Twenty year earlier, a slightly different version of this service had also been the last regular steam-hauled train through the town.

However, the 1980s saw positive developments, with the most far-reaching being the re-opening of the Penistone line to passenger trains in May 1983. This began as the experimental diversion of the existing Sheffield-Penistone-Huddersfield service under a new set of rules, allowing it to be closed quickly if it was deemed a failure. The more direct Penistone-Sheffield line was under threat of closure and diverting these trains via Barnsley was seen as the only way of keeping the Sheffield-Huddersfield service alive. In the end, the line survived two closure threats, and, subsidised by both South and West Yorkshire's transport authorities, it has prospered enough so that stations at Silkstone and Dodworth have been brought back into use.

Two years later, in 1986, British Rail began a direct Barnsley-London service using one of its relatively new High Speed Trains. These 125mph trains need specialised maintenance, which had to be carried out in Leeds. Each morning three or four trains needed to transit from there

Fast forward thirty years and the scene is a different one. The shed is gone and the station now has a second platform. In the major reorganisation of 1959, the new Sheffield-Barnsley-Wakefield-Leeds diesel train service was launched and Court House station closed, all services now concentrated here instead. In the late 1980s British Rail experimented with a Barnsley-London service using High Speed Trains and one is pictured here leaving for Sheffield and St Pancras. Alan Whitehouse

This is one of the hourly Leeds-Sheffield trains leaving Exchange station in the late 1970s. It shows a scene now totally changed, with the old station before reconstruction, the bingo hall and bus station.
Bob Green

to Sheffield in order to form services to London. The idea was to put this downtime to good use by running one train via Barnsley instead of a slightly more direct route, to pick up fare-paying passengers. The service lasted less than three years, but after the railway system was

A train which few Barnsley people ever saw, but which affected many lives, was the daily newspaper service from Manchester which ran via Penistone and Barnsley before going on to Doncaster and Cleethorpes – an echo of some of the passenger services which ran in steam days. The train paused for a few moments at around 2.30am to detach a couple of vans, which were unloaded and the loads distributed in time to reach the town's breakfast tables. The locomotive is a Class 37 from Wath depot. Alan Whitehouse

privatised, the Midland Mainline train company tried again, this time using smaller trains which cost less to run. At one point there were three trains per day to and from London, although these were all withdrawn in 2008. Even so, it could be argued that today Barnsley has some of the best rail services that it has ever seen, with direct trains to Sheffield, Leeds, Huddersfield, Chesterfield and Nottingham.

The old Exchange no longer exists. The station was demolished and completely rebuilt in 1992 as part of a scheme to create a new transport interchange, combining trains with buses. The complex was rebuilt yet again, as part of a bigger redevelopment scheme, which

A classic shot of Exchange with a Class 114 diesel unit standing in the original platform. These were some of the first diesel trains built by BR as part of the modernisation plan and, by the time they were scrapped, were among the oldest on the network. The picture was taken in 1981. Vaughan Hellam

opened in 2007. The old buildings were carefully demolished and part of the structure transferred to the Elsecar Heritage Centre, where the footbridge that once linked the two platforms has been brought back into use.

The last goods traffic into Barnsley was a daily parcels service, which consisted of a single van attached to the back of a diesel unit at Sheffield. The service terminated at Barnsley and the diesel unit then carefully shunted the van into a siding at the north end of the station. BR used to operate a full collect-and-deliver parcels service using road vans to achieve a door-to-door service. But it was uneconomic and was axed in 1981. Andrew Walker

Sheffield-Llandudno- Summer holiday service was among the last of the holiday trains to survive and these two pictures show it arriving at, and leaving, Barnsley. BR once had a network of these services but the rise in car ownership and changing habits of holidaymakers spelled the end. They also tended to be slow, making them uncompetitive.
Andrew Walker/Bob Green

The Poole-Bradford service also ended its days in the 1980s. BR was under pressure to save money and running trains like this one meant having locomotives and carriages available for just a few days a year. Here, it is being hauled by a Class 45 diesel – the direct successor to the Jubilee and Black Five locomotives we have already seen.
Andrew Walker

During the 1990s plans were drawn to completely rebuild Exchange and integrate it with a new bus station. Passenger lifts replaced the old footbridge while the buildings themselves were demolished brick by brick and stored in the hope the they can one day be rebuilt at the Elsecar Heritage Centre. Standing in the new station – renamed Barnsley Interchange – is a Class 222 Meridian train operated by East Midlands Trains, one of the post-privatisation rail franchise operators. Like BR before them, EMT decided a Barnsley-London service was a good idea and launched in 1988. It lasted until 2009.
Bob Green

Ex-LMS 2-6-2 tank engine 41274 of Royston shed arrives at Court House, probably with the Cudworth Flyer. This operated as a push-pull service so the locomotive stayed at the same end of the train, pushing the coaches back to Cudworth. D Thompson/Author's Collection

A typical Court House scene: an Ex-Midland Railway 4F loco, No 44446, stands with a train to Chesterfield. The plate on the smokebox door reading '55D' tells us the locomotive was allocated to Royston shed.
J Sedgwick/ARPT Collection

It is Winter 1955 and you can almost feel the cold as a little knot of people on Platform 2 await the arrival of a local train, probably from Sheffield. Although it was to close only four years later, Court House was rebuilt that year, the old roof going and being replaced by new platform canopies. B A Jordan

Conditions are rather better in this view taken before the rebuilding work began. Locomotive 40193 is another example of the fleet of 2-6-2 tank engines the LMS railway built for local passenger work. Bob Green

It is now 1957 and the rebuilding work is finished as Class C14 locomotive 67448 stands with a local train. These 4-4-2 tank engines were built to an essentially Edwardian design by the Great Central Railway and gave fifty years or more service. Barnsley shed always had a trio of them to hand for working local passenger trains. J Sedgwick/ARPT Collection

Diesel trains began making their appearance in Barnsley from 1958. One of the new trains, later known as Class 114, stands at Court House waiting to leave with a service to Sheffield. Author's Collection

A **final look** at Court House with this splendid shot of Royston shed's 41274 arriving with a train from Sheffield Midland. The year is 1955 so Court House is in its original condition. Many people would say that this was the better station of the two – less draughty and more comfortable with better facilities. Alas, four years later, it would close for ever. B A Jordan

CHAPTER SIX

GO WEST

As Barnsley's railway system took shape, the obvious missing link was a route to the west, towards Penistone and the main line across the Pennines from Manchester to Sheffield. There was no shortage of candidates willing to build it and the first proposals were put before parliament as early as 1842, although it was to be another seventeen years before the dream became reality.

Many of these early schemes were far more ambitious than merely linking Barnsley with Penistone. The Barnsley Junction Railway wanted to link the main line at Penistone with the North Midland Railway at Royston, passing through Barnsley on the way. The town – and the region's – railway history might have been very different had this project gone ahead. But it was rejected four times, even though a modification to take the line from Barnsley via Monk Bretton to the North Midland line at Cudworth was substituted for the original route. Eventually, this piece of railway, or something very close to it, was built by the Midland Railway to link Barnsley with Cudworth.

Six years later, the Manchester, Sheffield and Lincolnshire Railway (MLSR) managed to obtain powers to build a line from Penistone, in the process defeating a rival scheme put forward by the South Yorkshire Railway. It speaks volumes for how important railways were seen in the mid-nineteenth century that all these companies were prepared to spend time and money squabbling over the rights to build a line of no more than 6 or 7 miles in length.

The MSLR might now have the Parliamentary powers to build its railway, but it was in no position to actually start work. Financially crippled by the cost of building the famous Woodhead Tunnel on its Manchester-Sheffield main line, it was now suffering from what would today be called a 'cash flow crisis'. The company came in for heavy criticism from coal owners, who were anxious to see a route to the lucrative markets of industrial Lancashire opened up as quickly as possible. It was only when the Great Northern Railway, a company which had no line into the town at all, threatened to launch its own Barnsley-Penistone proposals that the MSLR was galvanised into action, dusting off its plans and starting work. It pushed eastwards stage by stage, with a colliery often being the next staging post, allowing a flow of traffic to begin to replenish the coffers before tracks were laid further.

There was a more lengthy pause after reaching the colliery at Dodworth, before the station at Summer Lane, on the western outskirts of the town, was opened as a passenger terminus in 1855. As the terrain then became more difficult with unavoidable curves and steep gradients, the MSLR pondered the best route to take before striking out and opening a goods yard off Regent Street, in 1857, which would eventually become part of the Court House station site. The job took another two years to finish, with a short link to Exchange station before a true Barnsley-Penistone passenger service could begin. More importantly, coal traffic from Barnsley and further south and east could now begin flowing over the Woodhead Line to Manchester.

The scale of the engineering challenge to make this happen can still be seen today. As Huddersfield-bound trains leave Barnsley, they begin a steep climb of around 1-in-50 on a sharp curve, passing through a deepening cutting that has been carved

We have already seen
4472 *Flying Scotsman* racing
through Stairfoot on the
1969 railtour which took her
through Barnsley. But disaster
struck leaving the town on
the homeward leg. The special
was routed to Penistone and,
on the steep climb towards
Summer Lane, 4472 stalled –
and could not be restarted. It
took a push from a Class 37
diesel – sent out from Wath –
to get the train moving again.
L A Nixon

Until a strike by footplate crew lost the traffic to road haulage, one key freight movement through Barnsley was the daily fish specials, carrying fresh fish from the Humber ports to markets in the north-west. These trains were treated like express passenger workings, given the best locomotives and crews and operated to a strict timetable. A Class B1 locomotive, 61247, is seen here pounding up the 1-in-69 gradient towards Summer Lane with the Grimsby-Manchester fish train in the summer of 1952. L A Nixon

In an earlier era, a K2 2-6-0 general purpose locomotive is pictures leaving Barnsley with a local train for Penistone. Manchester Locomotive Society

through rock. The gradient does not ease much until Summer Lane has been passed. As with most lines, it was originally built with just a single track, which was quickly found to be inadequate for the number of trains wanting to use the new route, resulting in it being doubled in 1871. Climbing towards Penistone, more engineering challenges are encountered, with a tunnel and curving viaduct at Oxspring before eventually reaching the town itself.

While coal was all-important, this was also a railway that handled general goods too. The Barnsley British Co-operative Society established a corn mill, jam factory, distribution warehouses and a dairy at Summer Lane, with house coal also being delivered there. Further along the line, a station was added at Silkstone in 1877 along with extensive carriage sidings for the seaside excursions and special trains that were an important feature of Barnsley's railways for many years.

While the route was never a grand main line, it did enjoy some prestige: a couple of its daily passenger trains ran all the way from Penistone to Cleethorpes and in the dead of night, a newspaper train ran from Manchester to Cleethorpes via Penistone and Barnsley, while a Saturday holiday train ran from Bradford to Poole in the summer. In later years, this service achieved a kind of fame by being the last service through the town to be regularly steam-hauled, a feature which ended in 1966.

Completion of the line cemented Penistone's status as a major junction. In addition to the Manchester-Sheffield main line, and the line to Barnsley, the Lancashire and Yorkshire Railway's route from Huddersfield also ran into the station. As these developments progressed, Penistone station was moved about half a mile east so that it sat astride this set of junctions.

In recent years steam has returned to Barnsley with a series of railtours using the Sheffield-Barnsley-Penistone line as part of their itinerary. Here, a BR Standard Class 4, 76079, and a Black Five, 45407, are caught passing the site of Summer Lane station.
Bob Green

At almost exactly the same spot but about fifty years earlier, a pair of Class J11 locomotives appear to be making good progress with an excursion train. The J11s were regarded as 'go anywhere, do anything' locomotives.
Steve Armitage Collection

Trains on the Barnsley-Penistone line split between local workings and long-distance services. A couple of trains each day ran between Cleethorpes and Penistone and Class B1 61112 has charge of what appears to be one of these trains passing Summer Lane in 1957. In the background are the vast Barnsley British Co-operative Society warehouses. Steve Armitage Collection

When complete it was an imposing five-platform station, which quickly acquired a reputation as the windiest place on the national railway network!

Key to this status was the construction of the Woodhead Line. Railway engineers had struggled for years to find a viable route across the Pennines before work began here in 1837. So too did the problems, however, with the project's first engineer resigning in despair at ever seeing the route completed. After this, Barnsley's most famous son, Joseph Locke, took over, though even he found building the line a major challenge, and by 1841 there were suggestions that it should be abandoned altogether. Locke refused to give up and by the following year had 1,000 men working on the Woodhead Tunnel. At 3 miles and 22 yards long it was, at the time, the longest in the country, although by the time the the national rail network was completed it had been relegated to third place. The Manchester, Sheffield and Lincolnshire Railway paid a heavy price for it: instead of the estimated £60,000, it had cost £200,000, using 150 tons of gunpowder and killing 26 men in the process.

It was 1845 before the tunnel was completed and special trains traversed the 3 miles of gloom under the Pennine hills. It is said that passengers on the first train broke into spontaneous cheering when they emerged once again into daylight. The company made a big mistake in not building a twin track tunnel from the start, because as

The same Co-op buildings also dominate this view. The locomotive is an ex-LMS 'Jubilee' class 45647, named *Sturdee*, which suggests this is the Poole-Bradford summer Saturdays holiday train. At the time 45647 was based at Farnley Junction, Leeds. L A Nixon

Summer Lane signalbox stood less than a mile from Barnsley town centre. Yet it had neighter mains electricity nor running water. It was lit by oil lamp and signalmen brought in their own water in plastic containers. The building was old even when this picture was taken in the early 1970s. It is a Manchester, Sheffield and Lincolnshire Railway MkI box and probably dates from the 1870s. L A Nixon

moving coal trains. At Dunford itself, yet more sorting sidings were laid in, this time to assist in sorting empty wagons heading back to their home collieries to be refilled. A tiny railway community was set up at Townhead, with rows of terrace houses which, even today, look as though they have been transplanted from the backstreets of a railway town and set down high on the moorland. It all transformed Penistone into something of a railway town. No locomotives were ever based there, but the station itself needed five signal boxes to control it, which alone provided around two dozen jobs. Half a dozen more signal boxes were required along the main line to Dunford Bridge and the Woodhead Tunnel mouth. Scores of shunters, wagon examiners and fitters were needed, as well as porters for the passenger station and managers to keep them all in line.

But for all its successes, Penistone also acquired a less enviable reputation: as the scene of fatal accidents. At the height of a bad run of fatalities, it was said that some nervous rail travellers would book their journeys by routes that avoided Penistone completely. In 1884, twenty-four people were killed when an axle broke on a locomotive hauling an express passenger train. All but the last carriage were flung down an embankment and smashed to matchwood. Less than six months later, in 1885, another broken axle, this time on a coal train, caused it to derail, which led to it derailing a Rotherham-Liverpool excursion train. Four passengers died on this occasion. The following year,

was so often in Barnsley's railway history, a single track quickly proved inadequate. This meant that a second tunnel had to be built, which opened seven years later. The traffic simply kept on coming, dominated by coal. At its busiest, around 100 trains were using it every 24 hours and it was estimated that 9 in every 10 were either coal trains, or empty wagons being returned to the South Yorkshire Coalfield.

It is little surprise then that Penistone also developed as a freight railway centre, with extensive sidings laid in between there and the junction with the Barnsley line. As the route climbed up towards the summit at Dunford Bridge, loop lines were laid to allow faster trains to overtake the slow-

Summer Lane station closed in 1959. By 1971, when this picture was taken, traces of the old station still remained. A Brush Type 4 (later Class 47) locomotive is, unusually, taking a load of full merry-go-round hopper wagons up the line from Barnsley towards Dodworth and Penistone. The usual flow was the other direction, with empties being taken this way and loaded trains returning in the opposite direction. Alan Whitehouse

As the line left Summer Lane the gradient changed – it is clearly visible in this shot – giving steam loco crews a chance to catch their breath. This is another fish train and one of Barnsley shed's Class N5 tank locos has been attached to give the train engine a helping hand up to Penistone.
L A Nixon

twenty people were injured when a string of carriages broke away from a train and ran back into buffer stops. Yet another axle failure in 1889 brought a Liverpool-London excursion train off the tracks. A few moments later, the London-Manchester mail train ran into the wreckage. Amazingly, only one person was killed in the resulting

tangle of wooden-bodied carriages. One more person died in 1887 when an engine ran into the back of carriages waiting to leave for Huddersfield.

By the turn of the century, the pattern of services for both the main line and the Penistone-Barnsley route had been set. Both were busy railways – the main line especially

so. And both led an untroubled existence until the late 1950s, when British Railways began taking a long, hard look at the routes and services it was operating. There was some good news: the main line through Penistone became part of a pioneering electrification scheme running from Manchester to Sheffield and also to Wath. This

A little further along the line was Dodworth station, sitting between the village and the colliery. This picture shows the original signalbox – a carbon copy of the one at Summer Lane – which was replaced by the brick structure that stands there today after a string of runaway coal wagons demolished it. The signalman had a lucky escape. *Heyday Publishing*

Down the years a succession of steam shunting engines and then diesels were employed at the colliery. In this 1978 picture, a former British Rail Class 04 shunter is positioning merry-go-round wagons. Merry-go-round, or MGR, was a system devised by BR and the NCB to load and unload wagons on the move – hence the term. The idea was to greatly reduce the number of wagons, locomotives and crew needed to deliver the same tonnage of coal.
Steve Armitage Collection

But Dodworth was also one of the last outposts of steam. Shunting tank engines like this one lasted until 1970. A Brush Type 4 locomotive waits for its train to be assembled.
Steve Armitage Collection

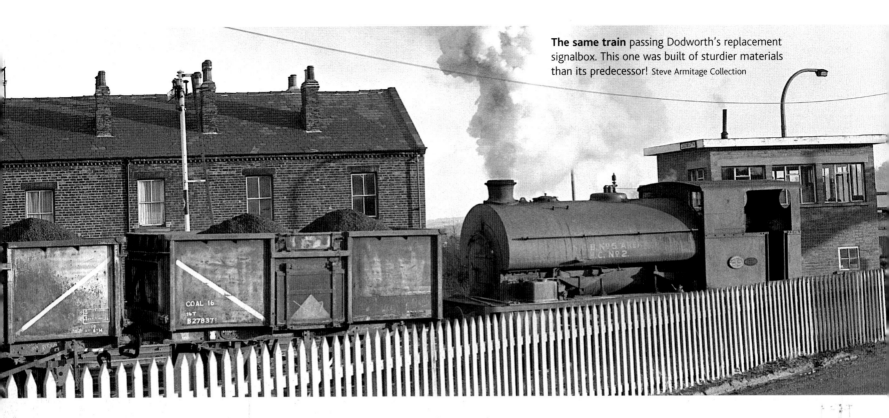

The same train passing Dodworth's replacement signalbox. This one was built of sturdier materials than its predecessor! Steve Armitage Collection

Dodworth's coal was mostly taken to Penistone and then on to Fiddler's Ferry power station near Warrington. But when the Woodhead Line closed in 1981 all this changed and the output went first to Wath and then along the Sheffield line to be taken to the power stations of the Aire Valley. Two Class 37 locomotives were always used on these trains and a pair are seen ready to leave. The signalpost exists today and can be seen from Dodworth's bypass! Bob Green

used a short section of the Barnsley line before heading to Wath via Wombwell, a line which will be described later. Electric trains began running in 1952 and the project was completed in 1955. Only four years later, the local services between Penistone and Sheffield and the Penistone-Barnsley-Doncaster trains were all axed in an economy drive.

The decision prompted anger in both towns. Many said at the time that the Penistone-Barnsley trains were well used and were certainly quicker than using the bus, although this was countered by the inconvenient site of Penistone station: most people using it faced a lengthy walk at the beginning or end of their journey. In the end Penistone kept passenger trains to Sheffield, but local stations along the way were closed. The service to Manchester also survived, but again with some local stations being axed. The Barnsley line became almost freight only, with the only exception being the nightly newspaper train. This still carried a passenger coach

Dodworth was one of the first collieries to be switched to the MGR system, with its distinctive hopper wagons. Most of the pit's output went to power stations, which is what the MGR system was designed for. But the theory that the trains never stopped moving certainly broke down at Dodworth where lengthy shunting moves saw the sets of wagons uncoupled, shunted, loaded, shunted and reformed before the complete train could depart. All this meant that the level crossing gates could be closed for long periods. The Hillman Imp car helps date these pictures to the early 1970s.
Tom Heavyside

Dodworth Colliery survived the miners' strike, but closed in 1987 as part of the relentless cost-cutting that decimated the mining industry. This pair of Class 37 locomotives from Wath depot are preparing to take over the final train, working it down to Barnsley, then on to Wincobank, near the present Meadowhall station, before reversing to head off to one of the Aire Valley power stations. Wath itself did not survive much longer, its reason for existing – moving coal – having all but disappeared.
Alan Whitehouse

on which the hardy traveller could leave Manchester at about 1.30am, arriving in the town a little over an hour later. And, as previously described, on Summer Saturdays the Bradford-Poole train ran over the route. However, neither of these services was of much use to locals.

When the M1 motorway was driven through Dodworth in 1967, the rundown of the route continued as part of it was reduced to single track after the cost of a double-track bridge was not thought worthwhile.

General goods traffic dried up just as it did across the whole of the railway system and, around 1977 – the precise date is uncertain – the Co-op ended deliveries of house coal to its depot at Summer Lane when the connection into its sidings was worn out. A replacement was not considered cost-effective, which left Dodworth Colliery as the last remaining source of traffic for the route.

Out on the main line, things were also going from bad to worse. Passenger services between Sheffield and Manchester were axed in 1970 after years of rumour and a hard fight by Penistone Town Council to have them retained. Instead, the Huddersfield-Penistone service was extended into Sheffield. But eleven years later BR closed the Woodhead Line completely, citing a decline in coal traffic, and the fact that the electrification equipment was worn out as the reasons. With

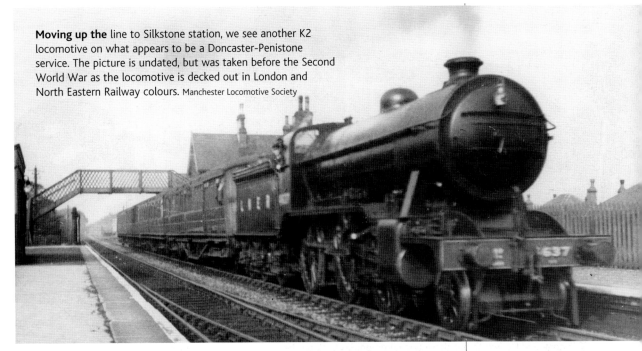

Moving up the line to Silkstone station, we see another K2 locomotive on what appears to be a Doncaster-Penistone service. The picture is undated, but was taken before the Second World War as the locomotive is decked out in London and North Eastern Railway colours. Manchester Locomotive Society

just eight passenger trains per day being the only traffic between Penistone and Sheffield, BR put this service up for closure.

A deal was struck in which the Sheffield trains would be re-routed via Barnsley. It would involve a longer journey from Penistone to

One of Barnsley's C13 tank engines brings a Barnsley-Penistone local train to its destination. The imposing signalbox is Huddersfield Junction. It is high because the signalman needed a good view across a complex set of junctions and sidings. The picture dates from the immediate post-war years: the engine has 'British Railways' on its tank sides, but as yet, there is no evidence of the overhead wiring associated with the electrification scheme of the early 1950s. L A Nixon

Silkstone lost its station when the passenger services were withdrawn in 1959 – but regained them when the service was relaunched in 1984. Huddersfield-Sheffield trains were diverted via Barnsley and new stations at Silkstone and Dodworth put these two communities back on the railway map. Alan Whitehouse

Penistone's early railway days were recorded by Biltcliffe's, the local photography firm. This picture, dating from the turn of the last century, shows Barnsley Junction, where the lines to Barnsley and Sheffield diverged.
Manchester Locomotive Society

Sheffield, but the alternative was complete closure. The line was brought back up to passenger standards in just seventy-five days, and the new service launched in 1983 after an eleventh hour deal was struck with South Yorkshire's transport authority, who agreed to subsidise the new service. The longer journeys from Penistone had to be offset against the new links between Barnsley and Penistone and Barnsley and Huddersfield. A year later, Silkstone station was re-opened, followed by Dodworth. The service was increased to offer

A Class 04 2-8-0 locomotive draws a lengthy mixed freight into Penistone from the Sheffield direction. Nine out of every ten trains on the Sheffield-Manchester Woodhead Line were coal trains. By now the overhead wiring is in place, new signals have been installed and electric locomotives are about to take over from steam. In the background can be glimpsed one of the new electric fleet on what is believed to be the first test run of an EM1 from Wath to Penistone.' Manchester Locomotive Society

a train every hour and this is essentially the service that operates today.

But, just as the passenger service restarted, so coal came to an end. The output from Dodworth Colliery was diverted to the new loading complex at Woolley and the final trainload left in December 1985.

The Woodhead Line has now ceased to exist through Penistone. A track was left in place between Sheffield and Stocksbridge for steel traffic, but the route around Penistone and to Dunford Bridge is now gone completely. The trackbed is part of the Trans-Pennine Trail while the new tunnel, built as part of the electrification scheme, has been converted to carry high-tension electricity cables as part of the National Grid. From being a railway centre, Penistone now offers not a single railway job. The one remaining line is controlled from Barnsley and the remaining part of the station is unstaffed.

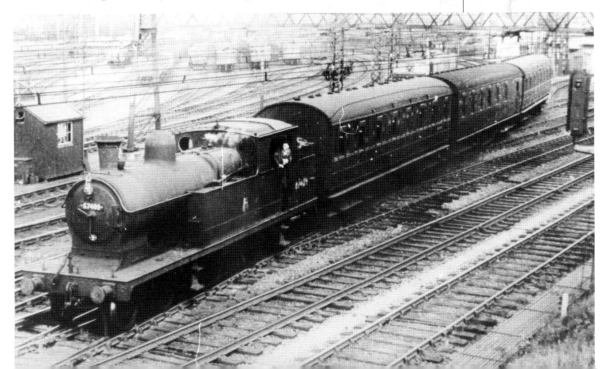

CHAPTER SEVEN

TEN MILE SLOG

When a road becomes too congested and traffic begins to pile up creating a jam, the obvious solution is to build a bypass around the bottleneck. This was exactly the situation faced in Barnsley as the coal traffic grew beyond anyone's expectations. New mines were being sunk almost constantly, and the coal they produced found a ready market.

This was a particular problem for the Manchester, Sheffield and Lincolnshire Railway. Their lines tapped into a growing number of collieries and their main 'export' route was to Penistone and over the Pennines to the thriving industries of Lancashire and the docks of Liverpool. The route through the town centre was simply becoming choked and unable to handle all the traffic on offer, especially when the coal trains were added in to the passenger and general goods trains.

A bypass was the solution, and so the Worsborough Branch was born, although the line was already partly in existence. After the discovery of a very high quality coal that burned with a fierce flame but left little ash, the South Yorkshire Railway had already opened a line from Aldam, near Wombwell, which penetrated Worsborough Dale, in 1850. Everyone had wanted

Penistone was in some ways the hub of the Manchester, Sheffield & Wath electrification scheme: The line from Manchester divided here with the main line running to Sheffield while the other route took the line to Barnsley and then diverged again to Wombwell and Wath. This 1954 view almost certainly shows a test run by No 27000, one of a class of seven electric locomotives built to haul express passenger trains.
J W Armstrong/ARPT Collection

The end of the daily Sheffield-Manchester service via Penistone did not mean the end of passenger trains: there was a steady stream of enthusiast specials including this one hauled by 76 049. Alan Whitehouse

The Woodhead line was electrified because of the heavy coal traffic which passed over it – mostly from Wath. Here, No. 26029, one of a class of 57 Class EM1 (Electric Mixed traffic type 1) locomotives heads coal empties through Penistone station.
J W Armstrong/ARPT Collection

By the mid-1970s the passenger service had been axed and the EM1 locos had been designated Class 76. No 76 003 heads a familiar set of coal wagons westwards at Huddersfield Junction. Tom Heavyside

The EM1 class were equally at home hauling passenger or freight trains – in fact some were fitted with boilers to supply steam for the carriage heating system – a hangover from steam days. No 26011 stands at the west end of Penistone station in 1954 with an express to Manchester. J W Armstrong/ARPT Collection

this new coal and the Dearne and Dove Canal provided the earliest form of transporting it. The canal ended at a basin at Worsborough, which is still there today. However, a railway was clearly the future and the SYR set about gradually extending their line along the dale, serving collieries en-route.

By 1875, the line had reached Strafford, Sovereign and Moor End collieries in the Dodworth and Silkstone Common area, and the original single track had been doubled. From Moor End, it was a short, but difficult, leap to reach the Barnsley-Penistone line about a mile beyond Silkstone Common. Around 2.5 miles of new track would be needed, but they would be on a severe gradient of around 1-in-40 and mostly on a curve. This increased the rolling resistance of wagons, which would travel through two tunnels, before making contact with the Penistone line at what became known as West Silkstone Junction.

The SYR had by now been taken over by the Manchester, Sheffield and Lincolnshire Railway. Its directors cannot have been very enthusiastic at the prospect of completing the missing link: the gradient would make it expensive and difficult to operate. But there was little option. The existing line through Barnsley was difficult enough with a 1-in-76 climb up from Stairfoot, which steepened to 1-in-50 between the town centre and Summer Lane. Banking engines that pushed from the rear were already needed, and this only slowed down operations and added to the congestion.

Once the link line was completed,

the whole route opened as a bypass around Barnsley in August 1880 with absolutely no formalities. This was a utility railway right from the start and had been built as cheaply as possible. It had no fewer than six level crossings (engineering the line to pass over or under roads would have been more expensive), and the final section was as punishing as the initial surveys had suggested, with gradients of around 1-in-40 and a short stretch of 1-in-37.

At various times the route served around a dozen collieries, though not all were open at the same time. At the lower end of the line, in the Worsborough area, there were sidings for local industries and at Worsborough Bridge there was a

The year is 1979 and the whole Manchester, Sheffield & Wath system is just two years away from closure. The main line side of Penistone station has been closed for over nine years – though a local Sheffield-Huddersfield service remained – and is beginning to look neglected as 76 046 rumbles through with a westbound coal train. Bob Green

After the line to Wath left the Penistone-Barnsley route it fell away rapidly on a 1-in-40 gradient from Silkstone towards Worsborough and Wombwell. Towards the top of the gradient were the two Silkstone Tunnels, notorious in steam days when four locomotives, all belching steam and smoke, needed to pass through them. No such problems for this pair of Class 76 electric locomotives heading up the gradient with a loaded coal train. L A Nixon

All trains coming up the gradient needed at least one banking engine at the rear, helping to push the train up the hill and prevent runaways. There were always several banking engines on hand at Wombwell Main Junction. They gave assistance as far as West Silkstone Junction at the top of the incline. L A Nixon

The steepest part of the gradient began at Wentworth Junction, where a small branch line ran off to Wentworth Silkstone Colliery. In steam days banking engines were based here. A Class 04 2-8-0 engine gets some attention from its driver. Bob Green

goods shed for local deliveries of general merchandise.

The line proved difficult to operate from the outset and around the turn of the last century, the Great Central Railway (successor to the MSLR), set about a reorganisation; classifying trains as either single or double loads and setting out a system of operation for each one. Every train needed at least one assisting engine, either at the front (a pilot engine) helping to pull, or at the back (a banking engine) to push. The heaviest double loads, which amounted to around sixty loaded wagons of

coal, needed both forms all the way from Wombwell. When the Wath Concentration Yard opened in 1907, trains operated from this point and started out with two locomotives before making their way along to Aldam Junction, then to the complex Wombwell Main Junction and finally onto the Worsborough Branch itself.

The initial section, as far as Wentworth Junction, was a relatively easy climb. But here another two engines were attached at the front and rear and the whole cavalcade moved slowly off; four locomotives working flat out. In

bad weather, the locomotives were prone to slipping as they struggled with the weight of each train and it was far from unknown for a queue to build up further down the line as trains waited their turn to tackle the final climb. On the climb itself, crews on the rear two locomotives found the two Silkstone Tunnels had been filled with smoke and fumes from the two leading engines and had to tie wet handkerchiefs around their faces to try to ward off some of the worst effects. All in all, it was an unenviable job, and much of it fell to footplate crews from Barnsley shed, which was

On a wintry looking day in 1947, a Class 04 locomotive eases its way cautiously down the incline approaching Wentworth Junction. Coming downhill was no faster than going up because the majority of freight wagons did not have a brake so the train had to be slowed by the locomotive and the guard in his brake van at the other end of the train. For steep inclines like this 1-in-40, a number of handbrakes on the wagons would also be applied, meaning the train then had to stop and wait while they were taken off at the bottom. H C Casserley

responsible for providing crews at Wentworth Junction.

In 1925 a huge new locomotive, the most powerful steam locomotive ever to run in the UK, was drafted in to help with the banking duties. This was known as the U1 class, a Garratt-type engine where two chassis are linked by a girder frame on which the biggest boiler possible is placed. It was disliked by footplate crews because of its size and unwieldiness, but it was capable of doing the work of two conventional engines. It spent the working week at Wentworth Junction, only returning to Mexborough shed for maintenance on Saturday evening. During the week, basic servicing was carried out in the open and the Garratt took coal at a specially constructed bunker in the pit yard at Wentworth Silkstone Colliery, which was linked by a short branch, about three-quarters of a mile long.

The problems of running this difficult piece of railway were almost constantly on the minds of the managers responsible. As early as 1910, the Great Central Railway looked at electrifying the route from Wath to Penistone, but the plan got

Electrification transformed the way the line was worked: instead of four locomotives, two were enough. Better still, the banking engines could earn their keep coming down the hill too, by assisting with a system known as regenerative braking, in which the electric motors became generators, slowing the train down and putting current back into the overhead wires which trains going uphill could then use. This is why this long train of coal empties has two locomotives at its head. L A Nixon

no further. A scheme for a more specialised banking engine was drawn out, but no action was taken. Then the London and North Eastern Railway, successor to the Great Central, drafted in the Garratt. At around the same time the LNER began looking at electrification

again, but this time for the whole of the main Sheffield-Manchester Woodhead Line, and the route from Penistone to Wath via the Worsborough Branch.

It was not until 1936 that the electrification project was approved, and then only because Government

funds were put in as part of a major job-creation programme to counter the economic slump of the 1930s. The Second World War intervened not long after work began, and it was 1952 before stage one of the project – from Wath yard to Dunford Bridge – was

The problems of getting heavy trains – mostly coal – up the gradient led the London and North Eastern Railway to base its unique Beyer-Garratt locomotive at Wentworth Junction. This loco was a true monster – in effect a pair of 2-8-0 heavy freight loco chassis back-to-back with a huge boiler slung between them. It was crewed mostly by Barnsley shed men who disliked it intensely. The Garratt would spend the working week at Wentworth Junction, returning to Mexborough on Saturday afternoon for maintenance.
H C Casserley

Around twenty-five years later it was all so much easier: EM1 locomotive E26040 glides down the hill with a freight train containing a number of wagons with brakes controlled from the locomotive, just like a passenger train. All effortless and much faster. The locomotive though, looks almost as dirty as a steam engine!
Alan Whitehouse

commissioned. It transformed the way the Worsborough Branch was worked: two electric engines not only did the work of four steam locomotives, but did it more quickly, with some trains now twice as fast as they had been with steam power, and with absolutely no physical effort from the crew. It was a similar story on the main line through Penistone, with all trains, from express passengers down to slow coal trains, moving more quickly and reliably.

The 57 new EM1 Class locomotives were purpose-built and capable of handling any type of train. They all had the ability to generate electric current when braking, current which was fed back into the overhead power lines and available for use by other trains. This helped to make

the whole system – known as the Manchester, Sheffield and Wath Lines – economical to run.

But, just as the line itself had been built as cheaply as possible, so the electrification scheme was carried out as cheaply as possible. On the Worsborough Branch the original signalling was largely left in place, along with the old gated level crossings. Before a train could move, all six level crossings had to be manned, making the line expensive to operate. Initially, this mattered little as there was a constant flow of traffic and these costs were spread over a large number of trains. Unfortunately, as the 1950s turned into the '60s, coal production began to decline and the number of trains thinned out. The process accelerated through the 1970s as traditional industries

either disappeared or reorganised themselves, switching from rail to road. British Rail and the National Coal Board tried to counter this with a new system for moving coal from pits to power stations known as 'merry-go-round'.

This used high capacity wagons which could be loaded and unloaded on the move. In theory, the train never stopped moving, making a continual circuit between pit and power station. Some of the electric locomotives were modified to work in pairs to handle these trains. A plan was devised to have two engines hauling and another pair banking along the Worsborough Branch. So, for about thirteen years, the branch became one of only two places on the national railway system where four engines could

The **regerative** braking system meant that almost all downhill trains had two locomotives at the head, to help with the braking effort needed. But unusually, this train, pictured at Hound Hill near Worsborough, has three locomotives, Nos. 76 030, 76 022 and 76 050.
Bob Green

be seen working one train. If the expense of keeping the line open by manning all those signal boxes could have been overcome, this would have been a very cost-effective way of moving coal.

Unfortunately, as traffic seeped away during the 1970s, and the line became less and less used, its history began catching up with it: the night shift was abolished to cut costs and by 1981, there were just seven trains per day in each direction timetabled to use the route. Things were little better on the main line and British Rail announced a closure plan, citing the high cost of running the line, the age of the locomotives and the overhead electrification equipment as the reasons behind it. Despite a bitterly fought battle against the closure, the last trains ran on 17 July 1981 and today the line forms

part of the Trans-Pennine Trail. As with so many of Barnsley's railways, it was built purely and simply to handle coal. When the coal disappeared, so did the need for the railway.

Until the line closed, every ascending train had a banking engine at the rear. On this occasion the duty is being performed by 76 040 and, just for a change, the load is not coal, but steel. Bob Green

Kendall Green was the first of a string of five level crossings as the line skirted around Worsborough Bridge and Worsborough Dale. Locomotive 76 040 approaches the tiny signalbox which controlled the crossing. Bob Green

Some of the Class 76 fleet were modified to work in pairs under the control of one driver. They could be identified by the cables and sockets under the windscreens. This pair is heading a train of coal hoppers from Ashburys in Manchester to Wath Yard. The date is 1975. Alan Whitehouse

Worsborough Bridge in steam days: These pictures were taken at Worsborough Goods depot between the level crossings at Worsborough Bridge Crossing and Glasshouse Crossing. They show a Class K3 2-6-0 and a Class O2 2-8-0, both heading west. The railway is long gone but the houses in the background are still there .... Brian Almond

The modified engines in the Class 76 fleet were converted mainly to operate 'merry-go-round' trains, which used special hopper wagons to carry coal from pit to power station. A pair led by 76 006 approaches Lewden Crossing with a merry-go-round working in 1977. Tom Heavyside

.... while bringing up the rear are 76 024 and 76 026, which will bank the train to West Silkstone Junction – a total of four locomotives on one train, one of only two or three places where this happened on the entire rail network. Tom Heavyside

Aldam Junction was the place where the lines from Wath to Barnsley and the 'bypass' route to Penistone diverged. It was once a busy place with four tracks to handle all the trains. By 1977 two of the four had been scrapped and virtually all the traffic through the junction took the Penistone route. This view shows 76 006 and 76 016 coming around the curve from Wombwell Main Junction and heading to Wath Yard with a train of coal empties. Tom Heavyside

A panoramic view of Wombwell Main Junction where exchange sidings – for swapping between steam or diesel and electric locomotives – were installed as part of the electrification scheme. The banking engines were based here, and in this picture a pair of bankers are parked in their siding while another locomotive, which has been assisting with regenerative braking coming down the incline, has just detached from the train and will move across to join the other banking engines, waiting for the next job. All now swept away with only the Trans-Pennine Trail left. Steve Batty

In the early days of the electrification scheme, the line and its locomotives were in great demand for enthusiasts' railtours. This early 1950's picture shows the first of the electrics taking over from a Class B1 steam loco. This engine – No. 26000 – was the first of the class and was loaned to Dutch state railways immediately after the Second World War. The Dutch were desperate for locomotives and it was a chance to get some operating experience with the new engine whilst the electrification scheme was being completed. Dutch railwaymen nicknamed the engine 'Tommy' after the British infantrymen who had helped to liberate their country. After 26000 returned to the UK, the name was officially conferred. The nameplates can be seen in the picture. RCTS Archive

There were always places that electric locomotives could not reach – when the wires ended so did the usefulness of an electric loco! These two views at Mitchells Main Crossing show a pair of Class 20 locos hauling a short train of wagons, probably being taken for repair, and a Class 31 heading a train of ballast wagons, possibly for a weekend maintenance session.
Gordon Turner/ARPT Collection

Diesel locomotives were also used on local workings – often known as 'trip workings' – bringing trains from pits and other industries to Wath Yard before being sent on their way. No. 37 226 passes Mitchell's Main Crossing in 1979 with the daily coke train from the Monckton coking plant. The diesel will leave the train at Wath where an electric loco will take over for the run over the Pennines to Northwich, Cheshire.
Gordon Turner/ARPT Collection

Hauling coal wagons is a comedown for this Class 45 locomotive – it was built for express passenger and fast freight work as part of the 1955 Modernisation Plan. By 1979 Intercity 125 trains had taken over and 45 012 has been downgraded to this trip working. The location is once again Mitchell's Main in 1979.
Gordon Turner/ARPT Collection

Class 47 diesels were the most numerous on British Rail and many of them were adapted with a special slow speed control to allow trains of merry-go-round hopper wagons to be loaded and discharged on the move. To do this they had to be able to keep the train moving at precisely half a mile per hour. This is a train of empties headed by 47 197 at Mitchell's Main. *Gordon Turner/ARPT Collection*

Class 56 locomotives were British Rail's second generation heavy freight engines and only made an appearance in the Barnsley area shortly before the electrified route to Wath closed. They were mostly used on merry-go-round workings. *Gordon Turner/ARPT Collection*

A final view of Mitchell's Main Crossing. It is immediately obvious how far down in the world this piece of railway has come – the long gantries for the overhead wiring are partly redundant because two of the four tracks have been removed. A Class 40 locomotive, 40 156, is hauling a very traditional train of 16-ton coal wagons. A steam locomotive would look equally at home on this train. Tom Heavyside

In addition to the marshalling yard, Wath was also the site of a depot built originally for the new electric locomotive fleet. This 1977 view shows four of them parked up and waiting for their next duty. Tom Heavyside

Wath Yard was the centre of operations for coal traffic in the Barnsley area. Completed in 1907, it was at the time the largest marshalling yard of its kind in the world and laid out to a precise pattern of sidings that allowed for quick marshalling. Trains were pushed over a hump and groups of wagons rolled down the other side under gravity to be diverted into a siding chosen by the yard controller. This meant that wagons from different collieries could quickly be grouped and coupled together to form a train for the same destination. By the time this picture was taken in 1977, hump shunting had ended and the yard was far less busy. Locomotive 37 123 departs with a set of coal wagons.
Tom Heavyside

In steam days, Mexborough shed was home to scores of locomotives. As already described, the LNER Beyer-Garratt locomotive was maintained here and is pictured in 1952, carrying the BR number 69999. The original plan had been to base the Garratt at Barnsley Shed, closer to where it would be working. But this idea had to be abandoned when it was found that the loco was simply too big to fit the tracks around the shed yard! K H Cockerill/ARPT Collection

CHAPTER EIGHT

LAST ROLL OF THE DICE

Barnsley's railway system was one of the most complex in the country. The West Riding as a whole system was dominated by three companies: the Midland Railway, the Great Central Railway and the Lancashire and Yorkshire Railway, while the few gaps left by the main players were filled in by smaller companies.

Perhaps the best known of these smaller companies is the Hull and Barnsley Railway, or the Hull, Barnsley and West Riding Junction Railway and Dock Company to give it its full title. The H&B Railway is best known for not quite reaching Barnsley itself: its three arms got as far as Stairfoot, Cudworth and Wath. But that is in some ways to miss the point. This was a railway intended to challenge the monopoly of the huge North Eastern Railway that controlled all the rail routes into Hull, and this had a stranglehold over the coal export business.

The H&B was therefore a latecomer to the railway scene. The first stirrings came in the 1870s from coal owners and other business interests concerned at the North Eastern Railway's monopoly position. Even Hull Corporation lent its support and by 1880, Parliamentary permission was granted, although it would be another five years before the new line was ready for business. Just getting to this stage had not been easy: the H&B cost £60,000 per mile to build, over twice the original estimate, making it one of the most expensive railways ever built. This was partly because unstable ground along the route meant that an extra tunnel was needed and also because, as the H&B was built after Railway Mania, it needed to cross lines that had already been built – with all the bridges and other works coming at its own expense.

Although Parliament gave permission for it to be built, a request for running powers over other companies' lines to places such as Sheffield, Leeds, Huddersfield, Halifax and Bradford were all refused, even though these access rights were a common feature of Victorian railway buildings. It left the new railway out in the cold; able to run over its own tracks but restricted in how it might develop traffic from elsewhere. Even a

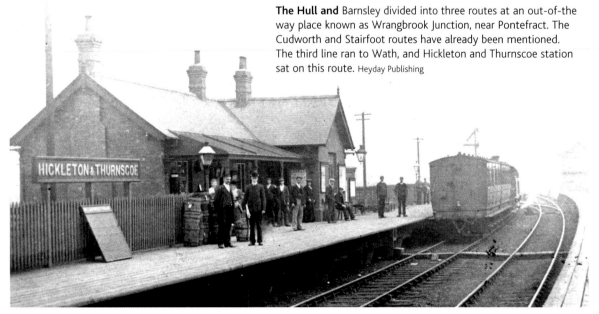

The Hull and Barnsley divided into three routes at an out-of-the way place known as Wrangbrook Junction, near Pontefract. The Cudworth and Stairfoot routes have already been mentioned. The third line ran to Wath, and Hickleton and Thurnscoe station sat on this route. Heyday Publishing

HICKLETON & THURNSCOE

The Hull and Barnsley Railway never got closer to Barnsley than Cudworth and Stairfoot. Passenger trains originally ran from Hull to Sheffield via Cudworth but these were axed in the 1930s. So this picture of a diesel unit on the H&B line at Cudworth is a rarity. It is believed to show a group of drivers setting out on a route-learning trip. Alan Whitehouse Collection

request for the rights to run into one of Barnsley's two passenger stations came to nothing.

The H&B's directors were reduced to pleading with the Midland Railway for access to its main line at Cudworth. The Midland agreed and a spur line was laid in to Cudworth station, where Hull and Barnsley trains ran from their own platform. In 1905, the Midland was generous enough to allow a passenger service to run over its tracks into Sheffield. But passenger trains were never a conspicuous success for the H&B and in 1932, the Sheffield service was abandoned, leaving only a local service between Hull and Howden. Another local service between Wath and Kirk Smeaton had been axed in 1929.

However, the new company had succeeded in setting up a railway to challenge the North Eastern. It had its own passenger terminus at Cannon Street, a goods station at Neptune Street, a locomotive workshop and, most importantly of all, a new dock, Alexandra Dock, for the export of coal. But it had come at a huge financial outlay: as soon as it began operating, the inevitable price war with the North Eastern Railway erupted, driving the Hull and Barnsley into administration just two years after it opened. It took two more years to come to a working arrangement and after this, the H&B's finances began looking up. A new line, built jointly with the Great Central Railway, gave access to more pits and the H&B jogged along until 1922, when it was finally taken over by the North Eastern Railway. This was just the prelude to a much larger reorganisation of the whole national

Along the Cudworth branch was Brierley Junction, where the Hull and Barnsley route formed a junction with the Dearne Valley Railway, another late entrant to Barnsley's railway network. Both these railways were about shifting huge tonnages of coal and that is precisely what is happening in this view, taken shortly before the line closed in 1966. The locomotive is an ex-LMS Class 8F. Alan Whitehouse Collection

This view, taken from Wrangbrook Junction signalbox, shows a wartime-built WD or 'Austerity' class locomotive with a guard's brake van in tow, doubtless heading off to collect another coal train.
Alan Whitehouse Collection

Parts of the Hull and Barnsley line were heavily engineered – this cutting, near Pickburn station, is the proof. The line's financial backers must have been confident of heavy and profitable coal traffic to have sanctioned this kind of investment. The locomotive is another WD 2-8-0 built for wartime service.
Alan Whitehouse Collection

railway system, and the following year, the North Eastern Railway itself became part of the even bigger London and North Eastern Railway.

The LNER began its own rationalisation programme, but the H&B main line was left intact, thanks to the buoyant coal export traffic. It was not until the 1950s, and the much deeper economy measures begun by British Railways, that the chill winds began to blow. Through the course of the 1950s, various parts of the system were closed, beginning with part of the Wath branch in 1954. The main line itself went in 1959 – a major year for rationalisation across the network as a whole – leaving just a few fragments that still gave access to collieries. The last part of the line at the Barnsley end, near Cudworth, closed in 1977. However, parts of the route around Hull are still in use to access the docks and there are no current plans to close them.

A second route which never reached the town, but had an impact on Barnsley's railway system, was the Dearne Valley Railway. This was another scheme based around the idea that a railway capable of shifting large amounts of coal quickly and cheaply would be a success. The DVR was one of the final railways to be built, and was constructed in stages between 1902 and 1908, running from a point just south of Wakefield to Edlington, near Doncaster. A set of junctions at both ends of the line gave access to other companies' routes and, unlike the Hull and Barnsley saga, there were few disagreements over this. The DVR, although an independent company, never owned any rolling

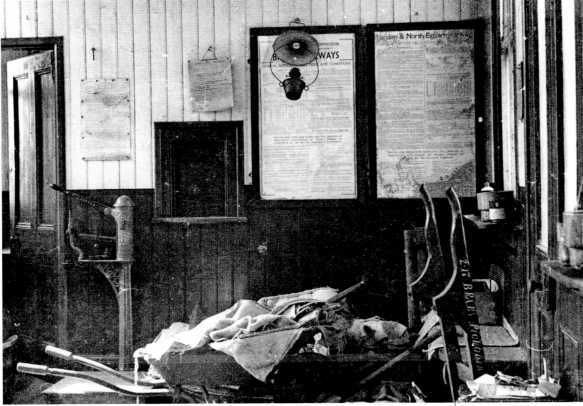

stock or ran any trains. From the outset it was operated by the Lancashire and Yorkshire Railway.

Coal was the key: this was a railway based entirely around the idea of offering collieries along the Dearne Valley an alternative outlet for their produce. And it was a success: by 1912 the original single line had been doubled and in the same year, a modest passenger service was launched from Wakefield to Edlington. And modest is the word: the trains themselves were almost always just a single carriage and the stations, at Grimethorpe, Great Houghton and Goldthorpe, were no more than an old carriage body for a waiting room and a single lamp. There was not even a platform, as the carriage had retractable steps

for passengers to clamber up and down. In truth, the service was little used except by pit workers getting to and from work and it was finally axed in 1951.

The key to the DVR's success was connecting to other companies' lines so as to allow the lucrative coal traffic to find the quickest and cheapest route. A junction was built with the Hull and Barnsley line and a system of junctions at Brierley allowed other connections to be made. The end came in 1966, when most of the main line was closed as part of yet another rationalisation scheme. Some fragments survived where they could be used as a more convenient access to a colliery, but with the 1980's collapse of the coal industry, even these are now just a memory.

If you ignore the wheelbarrow, then Sprotborough station looks ready for its next passenger. But appearances are deceptive. The last passenger service ran in 1903. But the tiny station was left as it stood until well into the 1960s – a real time capsule!
Alan Whitehouse Collection

ACKNOWLEDGEMENTS

It is now over 25 years since the first 'Rails through Barnsley' was published. In that time new pictures of Barnsley's railway system have come to light and history itself has moved on – the railway system has changed and – unfortunately – contracted even more in that time as coal mining has finally become a thing of the past not just in Barnsley, but across the South Yorkshire coalfield.

So this book has only a little in common with its predecessor. Some of the pictures are the same, but only where they are necessary to properly tell the story. In the main, new and often previously unseen pictures have been found which hopefully will give a completely new slant to the story.

So, grateful thanks must go to all the individual photographers who have contributed to this book. And to those who guard the collections increasingly held by railway societies and trusts. Without their help, this would have been an impossible job.

Some individuals need personal thanks and in no particular order, they are Steve Armitage for assistance with digitising and enhancing some images. Dr L A Nixon, one of the country's most prolific railway photographers also readily agreed to assist, as did Tom Heavyside. The Manchester Locomotive Society, Armstrong Railway Photographic Trust and Old Barnsley opened their archives and generously allowed material to be used. The story of Barnsley's railways moves constantly on and both Andrew Walker and Vaughan Hellam recorded the changing scene through the 80s, 90s and 'Noughties'. Their work has been a great help in bringing the story up to date.

Andrew Walker's maps show clearly how the system expanded –and then contracted. Andrew Walker and Keith Long read the manuscript spotting errors and making suggestions. Andrew Walker read the proofs, combing out many mistakes between them. Bob Green of the Railway Correspondence and Travel Society was quietly encouraging at a time when the project was not going well.

But mistakes do, inevitably, creep in. These are my responsibility entirely. Every effort has been made to correctly attribute each picture and to check each fact. If I have fallen short of the ideal anywhere in this book, then my apologies are due.

Alan Whitehouse